Praise for

THE TEACHER WHO COULDN'T READ

People tend to look at others who have overcome physical tragedies and call them courageous. For John Corcoran to openly admit his life-long struggle with illiteracy took more courage than my battle with cancer. This book touched me personally because I know the mental challenges in life can be greater than the physical. The value of his story is that it leaves us with hope. — *Dave Dravecky, ex-professional baseball player*
with the San Diego Padres and the San Francisco Giants,
author and speaker

Although John is my uncle, I never knew he was illiterate. It's unbelievable what he did to get by. The start of solving every problem is exposing it, and this book should wake us up to the astounding problem of illiteracy. I thank him for what he has taught me.

— *Bo Eason, All-American, defensive back*
with the Houston Oilers and professional actor

The Teacher Who Couldn't Read is an eye-opening account of John Corcoran's five decades of shame and confusion as he tried to function in society without even basic reading skills. This book is disturbing in the truths it tells about how easily a person can fall through the cracks of our education system. — *The Honorable Paul Simon*
U.S. Senate, Illinois

John Corcoran has become a champion in the literacy movement in America. He has suffered the pain, humiliation, and consequences of illiteracy. His courage and vision helped him overcome the odds. His is an inspirational story and is must reading for those who believe literacy is a key to America's future.

— *Jim Duffy, ex-president of ABC TV network*
and co-founder of Project Literacy U.S.

When I heard that John Corcoran had been illiterate, I couldn't believe it. He was my freshman coach and taught us basic principles of good sportsmanship. This book is more than the story of illiteracy, it is a great example of the power of setting goals and the drive it takes to succeed. — *Willie Buchanan, former student,*
National Football League all-pro defensive back,
Green Bay Packers Hall of Fame,
youth minister at his church

Your book will provide hope to those adults still struggling to acquire the basic literacy skills. Your experience demonstrates that it is possible to learn to read and write at any time in one's life, if one has the desire and perseverance to do so. Your words paint a very clear picture of the pain and frustration suffered by those who are unable to develop their full potential.

— *Jinx Crouch*
President of Literacy Volunteers of America

John Corcoran is doing a great service in revealing his own pain and progress. His story is not only fascinating and challenging, but also stimulates us with solutions.

I think first it is a poignant and passionate personal exposé. Although I do not agree with all the statements made by the author, they represent a personal opinion to which he is entirely entitled.

It is truly the best life-story presentation of a learning disabled person that I have read. It is written at a high-interest level and it captures and holds the reader's attention throughout.

John Corcoran has given us a visionary statement wrapped in his life story. John's vision is of a world that has the insight and thoughtfulness to check every child for reading ability. Do it early and without shame. Everywhere we hear human resources are our most important asset. That's simply not true if we are not taking every step to promote literacy and ensuring a fair and measurable chance for all who don't get it the first time.

This story is must reading for those teachers and parents who live with children who have not learned to read and spell. Quite often these children are bright and motivated, but they, like Mr. Corcoran, are dyslexic. While he shares the humiliation of his "hidden handicap," John offers hope and inspiration that one can succeed with strong family support, teachers who care, and appropriate reading instruction.

John Corcoran's courage in revealing his inability to read and his long search for help should reassure and encourage thousands who are devastated with learning disabilities. It is also a most powerful narrative for their loved ones too.

the
teacher
who
couldn't
read

JOHN CORCORAN

the teacher who couldn't read

KAPLAN
PUBLISHING
New York

Published by Kaplan Publishing, a division of Kaplan, Inc.
1 Liberty Plaza, 24th Floor
New York, NY 10006

Library of Congress Cataloging-in-Publication Data

Corcoran, John, 1937 Dec. 5-
  The teacher who couldn't read / John Corcoran.
    p. cm.
  Originally published: Colorado Springs, Colo. : Focus on the Family, 1994.
  ISBN 978-1-4277-9830-5
  1. Corcoran, John, 1937 Dec. 5- 2. High school teachers--United States--Biography. 3. Literacy--United States. I. Title.
  LA2317.C635A3 2008
  373.110092--dc22
  [B]
                          2008025253

Printed in the United States of America

2008
10 9 8 7 6 5 4 3 2 1

ISBN-13: 978-1-4277-9830-5

Kaplan Publishing books are available at special quantity discounts to use for sales promotions, employee premiums, or educational purposes. Please email our Special Sales Department to order or for more information at kaplanpublishing@kaplan.com, or write to Kaplan Publishing, 1 Liberty Plaza, 24th Floor, New York, NY 10006.

DEDICATION

*Dedicated to my dear friends who so generously shared
their precious gifts of literacy with me:*

Lynda Jones
retired director of the Carlsbad Library Adult Learning Center

Eleanor Condit
my volunteer tutor

the late
Pat Lindamood
a pioneer reading researcher and my master teacher

Kathleen Maria Corcoran
my beloved wife and teacher

CONTENTS

ACKNOWLEDGMENTS

I WOULD LIKE TO acknowledge the following people for their continuous support and commitment to a literate America, for their confidence in me, and for what they have generously given to foster our "noble cause."

New Adult Readers

the late Ed Anderson

Marianne Arling

Nanci Bell

Rodney Bell

Former President George H. W. Bush and Barbara Bush

Virginia and the late George Carey

Carlsbad City Library

the late Carole C. Carlson, who gave her time and talent to this book

City of Carlsbad, California

Former President Bill Clinton and Hillary Rodham Clinton

Rev. Donald Colhour

the late John Conway

the late Helen Copley

my son Johnny Corcoran

the late Randolph Crossley

Patricia B. Crisafulli

Jose L. Cruz

Stoney and Gloria DeMent

James Duffy

the late Phyllis Lindamood

Dr. Tim Lindamood

Joan McNichols

my agent Doris S. Michaels and her assistant Delia Berrigan Fakis of the DSM Literary Agency

my daughter Colleen Mertes; my son-in-law Todd Mertes; and my grandchildren Kayla, Stephanie, Bradley, and Jace

The National Institute for Literacy

Rotary International

San Diego Council on Literacy

Dr. Ann Schafer

the late U.S. Senator Paul Simon

U.S. Senator Alan R. Simpson and Ann Simpson

Gary Smith

Michael Sprague and Kaplan Publishing

Robert Sweet

Fran Thompson

Pamela and the late Dale Truax

Vince Walters

Michael Vezo

The Teacher Who *Can* Read — Revisited, 2008

FOR MORE THAN 20 YEARS, since first going public with my story as an adult learner, I have given 600 speeches and presentations, in front of large audiences and small groups, in the U.S., Canada, and in Europe. I have appeared on national, regional, and local television, and I've been interviewed by numerous newspapers and magazines. Each time, I tell the story of "the teacher who couldn't read." After all, that's what grabs the headlines. In the midst of my personal story, I make sure I bring home the point that really matters, the one that I want to make sure everyone gets. I'll say it here, upfront, to make sure you do too: *It is as important in America today to teach an adult how to read as it is to teach a child.*

I also emphatically state that we must reach children during that critical time frame between kindergarten and third grade. Once they get beyond third grade, an important window of opportunity closes as direct reading instruction is de-emphasized. The academic material gets much harder. The transition from "learning to read" to "reading to learn" has begun. Therefore, just as children are required to have physical examinations and immunizations before they start school, I believe they should also receive existing longitudinal-proven diagnostic tests for vocabulary development and reading readiness. Once their level of oral language processing and reading skills are ascertained, teachers can use screening results with instructional prescriptives to help each child acquire the basic skills to become a good reader.

We know that some children take to reading effortlessly, like ducks to water. Others will have some difficulty, and for others it will be even more of a challenge. Research tells us that, with proper instruction, virtually all learners can be taught how to read. Once they have the basics, we need to make sure they are motivated to learn with information, monitoring, and great books in the library for them to read. Just as with any new skill, reading is improved with practice. Our schools and literacy programs need books and articles that learners can read successfully in order to develop and grow.

Now, as a literacy advocate with two decades of speaking, presenting, and even testifying before Congress, I'd like to wind up into the real pitch. I want to tell you how reading is the cornerstone of all formal education; how there is no real equal opportunity for success in the classroom without literacy skills. Compulsory education requires public schools and public school teachers to accept all students, wherever they are, and to impart reading values and skills. It is a challenge that we can and must meet.

Then I picture in my mind a scene, one I've witnessed so many times before. When I'm addressing an audience—whether of teachers, parents, literacy advocates, policymakers, business leaders, or community members—my wife is sometimes present. Kathy, to whom I've been married for 43 years and counting, listens attentively, even though she knows this story as well as I do and perhaps even better. When I get too preachy, when I start to pound the statistics, she gives me a little hand signal, which means "Just tell the story, John."

In this book, I tell the story — my story — of John Corcoran, a little boy who went to school like every other child, innocent and eager to learn, and who over the years became "the teacher who couldn't read." And I'll tell of what it took, at the age of 48, at the Carlsbad Public Library Adult Learning Center and with the help of a 65-year-old volunteer tutor named Eleanor Condit, to finally learn how to read. As you'll read in this book, I worked with Eleanor for 13 months, after which I was reading at about a sixth-grade level. This was an extraordinary accomplishment for me — a grown man — who had gone nearly five decades of life without being able to write a simple sentence or to do more than pick out a few basic words.

From my tutoring with Eleanor I graduated to more intensive instruction: the Lindamood-Bell Reading Clinic in San Luis Obispo, California, where I was given a battery of diagnostic tests that uncovered a severe auditory discrimination problem. I was blessed beyond belief to be a student of Pat Lindamood, herself — my teacher and my friend. Pat taught me using a multisensory approach on how to decode the written word. Nanci Bell introduced me to the concept of visualization and verbalization to help me increase my comprehension. After hundreds of hours of instruction at the clinic, I was reading at the 12th-grade level.

It would have been fine with me and certainly with my wife if, in the beginning, I took my newfound literacy skills and joyfully used them without getting on a soapbox. Maybe I could have appeared at a fundraiser for the library's Adult Learning Center, or perhaps I would have tiptoed away quietly, my "secret" secure. No one would have to know who I was: the teacher who couldn't read.

But it hasn't happened that way, not the first time when, in 1994, *The Teacher Who Couldn't Read* was first published, and now in 2008, with the reissuing of my autobiography by Kaplan Publishing, along with the publication of my new book, *Bridge to Literacy: No Child—or Adult—Left Behind.*

I share my story with the hopes of educating others about the problem of illiteracy in America. My intention is also to inspire others, including those who cannot read or who have family members—especially children—who struggle with literacy. The moral of this story is simple, but powerful: *It can be done. Everyone can learn to read—including those of us with severe difficulties.*

As I have shared my life publicly, what remains the hardest part for me is to talk about teaching schools for 17 years even though I did not know how to read. Teaching school all those years was a greater moral dilemma for me than anything else in my life. It is not only embarrassing for me, but also for other teachers and for the teaching profession. With that baggage in hand, I've also gone public as an advocate for nonreaders, including generations of children who did not get from teachers and from schools what they needed to succeed. I don't condemn anyone: not teachers, parents, or schools. Rather, I just point out things the way they are: There are millions of people in America who do not have the literacy skills they need, especially in today's demanding, technologically advanced society. And we have more students being pushed along through the system who will either drop out or be given a high school diploma that doesn't mean much more than mine did all those years ago.

As I re-read these pages, which were first published just five years after I learned to read and write, I see the evidence of the emotional and spiritual healing that had begun then and still continues. There are places in this story where the rough edges are not smoothed, where the rawness of having spent decades in the subculture of illiteracy shows through. With the benefit of the years that have passed since then, I do see the entirety of my life in a different light. I understand now what it meant to become an emerging literate as I was in those early days, and then to fully join the dominate culture of the written word. But my intention is not to sugar-coat my story now, any more than it was then. My story *is* my story, honestly presented here.

I picture my wife Kathy with that little hand signal of hers again. *Just tell the story, John.* So here it is:

I remember a day clearly, even though it was nearly 20 years ago. I was driving my granddaughter Kayla, who was a third grader at the time, home from school. It was a couple of years after my work with the Lindamood-Bell clinic, but I was still advancing my comprehension. What challenged me at the time was the visualization and verbalization concept that I had learned, but which did not come easily to me at first. I had read a couple of novels, but I did not have the experience that Nanci Bell said all good readers have: that is, when they read, they see a "movie" in their heads. Good readers do this automatically, she said. How I wanted to be a good reader and have that same movie playing in my brain. So I asked my little granddaughter if she had that experience.

"*Of course*, Grandpa!" she told me.

I felt such joy over her answer, first of all because my little granddaughter was a good reader. Second, this child validated an experience that I was still grasping to master. I wasn't a true believer in this visualization and verbalization as yet. But when Kayla told me it happened to her, I knew my question was really a rhetorical one: *Of course* good readers visualize what they're reading. And, *of course*, with some more direct instruction in visualization and verbalization I would eventually get to that same point of comprehension mastery.

Today, when I read for pleasure, I do see the movie in my head. Not only do I picture the character, but I notice the details of whether he's wearing a red shirt or she's driving a blue car. I visualize and I verbalize. Words do paint pictures.

And pictures also inspire words. As I look at the cover of this book, which my new friends at Kaplan have created for the reissuing of my autobiography, my eyes are drawn to the man who is walking across the page. The man is so small and the book is so big. I know I am that little man, and I've been walking in this book for more than 20 years, since I first learned to read.

As I look at the little man on the big book, I'm also reminded what a challenge this is, personally and collectively. As a nation, collectively we face a crisis of illiteracy. We have the research that tells us what we must do; now we must have the courage and commitment to implement it. Personally, the challenge is telling a story that is at once so typical of adult learners and also so difficult to share. Once I made the decision to go public, I went forward fearlessly. But there have been many times — including very recently — when I have been hurt, stifled, and tripped. It's like being a boxer and taking a body blow. Many see a bloody nose and a split lip. Only the boxer feels the pain in the stomach or the ribs. Nor does that boxer want anyone to see that a blow has set him back on his heels. But he still feels it.

In every audience, no matter how polite and receptive, there are the cynics. They are the ones who question me about everything from whether I really didn't know how to read to my motivation for going public with my personal story. I want to tell them, "Hey, I'm a good guy! I want to improve the quality of life for other people." But I can't stand up there and say that because that would make me seem all the more unbelievable. So I listen to the questions and I answer them the best I can. And, I tell my story.

Just as this Introduction was being written, I was asked to speak to a local group, which is both a service and social organization. I didn't know much about the group, but since they were local, I agreed to be their speaker. My wife accompanied me to the event on a weekday evening. At the start of my presentation, I showed an eight-minute tape of an interview I did with Oprah. I have found over the years that this really grabs the audience, partly because the interviewer is Oprah, to be sure. But she also brought out my story in a thoughtful and emotionally powerful way, with images of me as a child, a youth, a teenager, and as an adult. As the videotape began playing, I noticed there was a lot of noise: rattling of dishes and conversation. Then after a couple of minutes, the room was silent.

When I spoke to this audience, which was mostly older people, they were very attentive and engaged. As I looked out at them, seeing people who were my peers, I wondered what my goal should be for the evening. Would I recruit some to become volunteer tutors? Would I alert them to the extent of the problem of illiteracy? Should they be on guard for reading difficulties in their grandchildren? I just let my story do the talking for me.

At the end of my presentation, a woman stood up and explained that she had raised four children. She had read to all of them before they started school, believing that this would help prepare them for learning. Her three older children became good readers right away. Her fourth child, however, struggled. She graduated from high school, but really couldn't read. Later she got help and went on to a community college where she received further instruction. Today, having mastered her literacy skills and receiving a degree, she works with deaf children.

I rejoiced in this woman's story, knowing how the experience of her youngest child also validated what I was telling this audience. We are out there — the adults who couldn't read. We go through 12 years of school with the best of intention, but at the end we still can't read much better than when we started.

Then I encountered one of the cynics. When he asked me his question, I could hear the edge in his voice. He wanted to know about the parents — where were they in all of this? If children aren't learning to read, aren't parents to blame? Yes, parents do play an important role in their children's reading readiness, I told him. But what about the parents who can't read or write? What about those parents for whom English is a second language, and who cannot help their children who were born here? What about children with so-called learning disabilities who need special instruction? In San Diego County, I told him, approximately 25 percent of adults have a deficiency in literacy. We have to take responsibility as a community in order to help these children.

I am not sure if my answer satisfied him, but I could tell by the looks and the nods in the audience that others heard what I had to say. What I didn't know at the time, however, was that one of the most important validations for me was happening back at the table where Kathy sat.

During dinner that evening, Kathy and I had conversed with a couple who looked familiar to us, but we didn't really know them. Come to find out, they were active in our church parish, to which Kathy and I have belonged for 43 years. Before my presentation, we had a nice, friendly visit.

After I spoke, the man confided in Kathy how moved he had been by my speech. He told her that he had read some newspaper articles by me and about me, but he had thought it was an "impossible story." He went so far as to say, "I thought this story was so impossible, this guy had to be a con man."

It's not the first time I've heard the "con man" comment, although I suppose someone who only reads a short article or who sees a few minutes of a television interview could be left with some doubts. Still, it gets my back up a little every time. What can I possibly say to satisfy these people? I can prove that I can read today. But how do I prove that until the age of 48 I couldn't read, other than to present my detailed story — with names, dates, and places — in a book.

Luckily, I had already convinced him of my sincerity. As he told Kathy, "When I heard John speak with such passion, I knew it was the truth."

The best way I can reach people — those who need help with literacy and those who are in a position to provide that help — is to tell the truth and to share my story. Now I am 70 years old, an age when many of my peers are spending more time on the golf course and at the beach, but I'm still at it: going wherever they will listen. I don't just go there as a speaker and as president of the John Corcoran Foundation. I also am a teacher.

Many times over the years, I've been asked the question: Are you still a teacher? No, I am no longer in the classroom. And for the record, I was not forced out. And no, they didn't know all those years that I couldn't read or write. I never had a negative evaluation and I never got caught. (If you want to know all the details, you'll have to read the rest of the book.) I was a teacher who did his best to create an oral and visual learning environment.

Just recently, after a television interview, I received an email sent by someone who found me via the John Corcoran Foundation website. She had been a student of mine many years ago. Here's a little of what she wrote:

" … You were my typing teacher and also my favorite! You always seemed calm and truly seemed interested in students learning… It's wonderful what you're doing for illiteracy!"

Oh, that did my heart good to read that. How kind of this woman to remember me after all these years and, after hearing my "secret" exposed on television, not to think ill of me. Being the "teacher who couldn't read" pains me, and every time I speak on this subject I feel like I'm going through another round of public confession of my sins and trespasses. Reading that email, I'm proud to know that one of my students knew that I cared.

I am by nature a teacher — just not in the classroom anymore. Every time I share information or an experience that educates, inspires, and helps others, I am fulfilling my mission. That's what the image on the cover of this book also conveys to me. The little man continues on his travels across the written word, a life journey if you will, from words that intimidated to words that empower. And I will tell my story again and again as long as there is an audience who will listen.

For the cause of literacy, I will continue to go out in public as the "teacher who couldn't read." But, thank God, today I am a teacher who *can* read. Now, I'll sit back and tell the whole story.

PROLOGUE

SECURITY WAS VERY tight that chilly November morning in Washington, D.C. As we approached the final checkpoint, I almost panicked. *Where is my passport? I know I had it in the hotel this morning. Did I leave it on the dresser? God help me; it must be here someplace.* My wife, bless her, was completely calm, standing quietly as I searched the pockets of my newly pressed suit. After fumbling for what seemed like an eternity, I found the passport, right where I had put it earlier.

Smiling with renewed confidence, I handed the vital identification to a stony-faced security guard. I wondered if he had taken a pledge, along with the ubiquitous Secret Service men, not to smile. What I did not know was that he *was* a Secret Service agent. He glanced at my picture, compared it with my Irish face, and reached around to open the gate. Finally, we entered the White House — not as tourists, but as guests of the president and first lady of the United States.

Unbelievable. Here I was, a fellow who five years earlier couldn't decipher the words in a second-grade reader, now one of nine presidential appointees to the National Institute for Literacy Board. The other eight men and women had advanced degrees or prestigious titles. After a nationwide search, the group had been chosen to implement the National Literacy Act, a challenging goal in an era when illiteracy is rampant. I was there as an emerging literate, speaking hesitantly, searching for words that were struggling to be released from my mind, words I knew were there, but somehow were buried like the passport in my pocket.

For weeks the FBI had probed every facet of my life. Neighbors who were casual acquaintances were quizzed by men with badges; business associates and professional people in our town were asked questions about my past and present. I remembered the traffic ticket I had received two years before and the lawsuits against my building and development company. Would those give me negative marks? Although the open book of my life had some smudged pages, I passed the investigation and my appointment was approved by the Senate just one hour before it adjourned. That was one test I didn't flunk.

Once inside the White House, we walked down a long hall, past an attendant who checked press badges and handed out news releases, into a small reception room. There, we were introduced to Secretary of Education Lamar Alexander, Supreme Court Justice Antonin Scalia, and First Lady Barbara Bush (who brought the president's regrets that he could not attend because his mother was critically ill). This ceremony marked the beginning of President Bush's dream for the National Literacy Act, and the end of his years as president. In two months he would extend to his successor, Bill Clinton, the challenge of achieving a literate America by the year 2000.

After an official photo was taken of us alongside Mrs. Bush (I could visualize it framed and displayed on my office wall), we were escorted into the Indian Treaty Room, a place where American history seemed to leap from the walls. A small, invitation-only audience stood up and applauded as we entered.

Mrs. Bush, wearing a simple blue suit and her trademark pearls, walked to the podium and smiled in my direction. (The fact that my six-foot-four frame towered over my colleagues might have had something to do with her focus.)

She stood behind the podium, knowing that this was one of her last official duties in the Bush administration, and said, "I admire all of you. You have the commitment to the urgent task to be done and have brought your varied gifts and knowledge to this work. What a wonderful legacy to leave to America."

I looked at my wife Kathy, smiling at me from the front row, and thought, *You helped me here, honey…you deserve the honor.*

We raised our right hands—*could anyone know how excited I was?*—and Justice Scalia administered the oath: "I [John Corcoran] do solemnly swear that I will support and defend the Constitution of the United States against all enemies foreign and domestic and I will bear true faith and allegiance to the same. I take this obligation freely without mental reservation or purpose of evasion. I will faithfully discharge the duties upon which I'm about to enter, so help me God."

I looked out at my family and friends in the audience and realized that I was standing in front of the room, at the head of the class.

It had been a long, risky journey, filled with pitfalls and detours, and I knew the future would bring greater challenges. But now, at last, I was armed with words. I had been set free from almost five decades of bondage.

*Reading helps us grow, head and heart. It gets children
ready for school and helps them do better once they get there.
It's a special time for children to be close to grown-ups who
care for them — a wonderful way to feel loved.* —Barbara Bush

CHAPTER I

A Little Child Shall Lead Them

KATHY COULDN'T MISS my noisy entrance. "Hi...I'm home,"
I shouted, as if that wasn't obvious. I tossed the book I was
carrying on the hall table and was immediately tackled by a little
blond tornado who wrapped her arms around my leg. Dragging up
the hall, impeded by a 30-pound weight, I pretended to ignore the
small body.

"Kath, where's Colleen? I can't find her anyplace."

With a squeal of impudent delight, my three-year-old princess
released her grip and fell on the floor. "Here I am, Daddy." She giggled as if we had never played this game before.

I grabbed her and we twirled around and around as all the frustration of the day began to melt. I felt like a cop who comes home
after putting his life on the line for eight hours.

Home was safety; no pretense, no moments when someone would
give me a suspicious glance or ask me to do an impossible task. I could
let my guard down.

Kathy stood on tiptoe to give me a kiss, at the same time slapping my hand as I grabbed a warm oatmeal cookie. It always amazed me how she managed to do three or four things at the same time.

"Supper's ready in about 15 minutes," she said, taking the cover off the Dutch oven to allow the mouth-watering aroma of pot roast laced with onions and vegetables to hit my senses. After teaching all day and coaching the basketball team after school, my appetite was like a bear emerging from his winter siesta.

With Colleen squeezed beside me, I sank into the brown leather recliner, ready for our nightly ritual of "reading" before dinner. "O.K., sweetheart, what'll it be tonight? Little Red Riding Hood? Goldilocks? How about Brer Rabbit?"

The big Golden Books and their wonderful pictures would stimulate my imagination to weave some crazy yarns. When I told the Three Bears, Cinderella, or another well-known fairy story, they were embellished with all the drama of Orson Welles or Alfred Hitchcock. Sometimes I could hear Kathy laughing in the kitchen at my tall tales. I had a lot of practice at storytelling.

Colleen had a surprise for me that night. "Read this, Daddy," she said, snuggling closer to me. She held out a new book, one with smaller pictures and more words. Her blue eyes were bright with anticipation.

"Well, now, what's the name of this book?" I looked at the first page, hoping there would be a clue.

"*Rumpelstiltskin*," called Kathy from the kitchen. "I've already read it to her at least ten times."

"What's it about, Colleen?" The other stories I knew from childhood or hearing Kathy read. All I needed to do was embellish them with a little drama. But this time I was stuck.

I turned the pages, trying to find something that would give me a hint. I looked at the first picture and started to weave a story, as I had done before. "Let's see...there's a girl...she lived in a house...and her father..." those were some words I guessed at, but nothing else made sense. Colleen was fidgeting, waiting for me to get on with it.

"Rumpel"...(I couldn't pronounce it)... "whatever her name... was a beautiful girl who lived in a house with her father." Pictures say more than words. So far, so good. "She sat at her spinning wheel all day long, making clothes for the King."

"Daddy, Rumpelstiltskin wasn't a girl...he was a funny little man." She knew the story too well to be fooled.

I couldn't decipher one word in this preschool children's book.

How I wanted to be able to read, to help her during those valuable growing-up years before school. Parents who can't read can't teach their children to read. My heart was wrenched, knowing that I could not give her what I didn't have.

Please, God, let her learn how to read, I prayed. *I don't want her to go through what I have experienced.*

"Let's see, the funny old man was really a prince in disguise," I began. Colleen squirmed; she wasn't buying this story.

"That isn't the way Mommy read it." She jumped off my lap and ran to her "treasure case," an old bookshelf I had painted red and white to match her room. On the top were her valuable possessions: a picture of the baby Jesus, two little yellow ducks, and some Disney characters. Lined up on the shelves below were her books, carefully placed in neat rows.

We had told her from the time I started bringing her books as presents, "Books are very special. Take good care of them." I knew their value, but not their contents.

When she brought me a book this time it was a familiar one. Safe.

Kathy called us for supper, but I noticed that her voice didn't sound steady. I put Colleen in her booster chair and sat down to savor my young wife's wonderful cooking. I thanked the Lord for the food, but when I looked up I saw that Kathy was crying.

"Kath, do all pregnant women cry before dinner?"

She continued cutting up Colleen's meat without answering me. I figured she must be fighting nausea and didn't want to talk.

Supper continued without conversation, except for "Drink your milk, Colleen." "Use your napkin." "No cookie until you finish your vegetables."

When we finished, I cleared the table and began to run water in the sink for washing. Kathy said she didn't feel well and was going to the bedroom.

After doing the dishes and putting Colleen to bed, I flicked on the TV. The news wasn't on and it was the wrong night for *I Love Lucy*, so I went to bed too. As I turned out the lights, I heard Kathy stifling sobs in her pillow. This wasn't like any other pregnancy upset.

"Kath, what's wrong?"

"Nothing," she sniffled.

Kathy was thinking, *I thought he was just a poor reader. That I could manage. But what will we do if he can't read at all? I don't want to be a full-time secretary all my life!*

It seemed easier to talk about it in the dark. I knew this was about my reading. "Don't worry about this, Kath. I do enough worrying for both of us. I think there is something wrong with my brain."

She didn't say anything.

Dear God, why can't I learn how to read? Why should Kathy suffer too?

Our little girl and the story of Rumpelstiltskin had revealed the fact that I didn't have just a slight problem with reading. I was illiterate.

Kathy realized for the first time that she had married a teacher who couldn't read.

*The happiest moments of my life have
been the few which I have passed at home
in the bosom of my family.* — Thomas Jefferson

CHAPTER 2

The Family

A RAP ON MY KNUCKLES with a fork meant "Don't reach across the table, Johnny." Our family may have been poor, proud, and penny-stretching, but Mama was a stickler for manners. We were taught how to use silverware just like rich people. "The salad fork goes to the left of the dinner fork, and the knife is on the right side of the plate with the spoons next to it," she would instruct us.

We were drilled on rules of table etiquette. *Never put a bottle on the table. Milk goes in a pitcher. Jam or jelly is taken out of the jar and put in a dish. Bread must be on a platter. Say, "Please pass." Don't talk with your mouth full. Don't leave the table until everyone is finished.*

Etiquette was the same whether we were living in a motor court, an abandoned convent, or a house with a real dining room.

I loved picking on my sister Judy, who was 18 months younger and wonderfully gullible. At the table I would whisper, "Judy, there's a mouse over there in the corner," and while she was distracted, I would drink her milk or grab her bread and jam. Sometimes my father would catch these little tricks and give me a wink. We men were outnumbered and had to stick together.

With five sisters, I thought I should be excluded from certain tasks, like setting and clearing the table or (*ugh*) washing dishes, but there was no reprieve. *Silly and boring*, I thought. Many years later at college I would be grateful for my etiquette training. I would be facing enough challenges; which fork to use didn't need to be one of them.

To say that my parents loved us unconditionally is probably incorrect. Unconditional love suggests perfect love, and my parents weren't perfect. But they were selfless and giving, no matter what the circumstances. All of us were fiercely loyal to one another, and at an early age we all assumed the roles of chief protectors and defenders of the Corcoran clan.

My mother's formal education was limited to high school, which she regretted, because she thought if you didn't have a college degree, you weren't bright. She believed that education equalled intelligence. Although she was well read and articulate — with particular interests in history, politics, and sports — she never considered herself smart.

"Someday, Johnny, you're going to college," she would tell me. "You'll learn more things than I ever did."

She wanted all of her children to earn college degrees. No exceptions. If she had known I couldn't read or write, she would have realized her dream for me was pure fantasy. But exposure to my mother's high expectations must have inspired me. Because although I didn't believe I could do it, I did. I credit my mother for part of that achievement.

When my mother was young, she was a fashion model — slender and attractive with a real sense of style. She always had good taste, and she insisted on quality or nothing. Long before discount stores and super sales, Mother could always find a deal. She also looked for the best in her family and expected the same of herself. But because her standards were so high, she also often felt she had failed.

With eight mouths to feed and eight bodies to clothe in a low-income family, she excelled in her ability to stretch a dollar. We didn't have much money, but she fixed us the healthiest meals she could. We didn't have a washer or dryer, but our clothes were always crisp and clean; they were scrubbed regularly, hung in the sun to dry, and ironed by hand.

Mother was everything to us: chief cook, keeper of the house, queen of the scrub board, teacher of etiquette, even weaver of an occasional dream. But her parenting activities left little time for fun or socializing. Mother and Dad built our family into a nomadic tribe, a closed community. We moved so often that there was rarely time to make good friends, and we also had certain rules that in a peculiar way isolated us. A major one was that we were never allowed to invite people to eat at our house. It took me a long time to understand that we couldn't afford it. We were not to eat at other people's houses, either. There was a sense of pride in good manners and upholding the family honor, even if our living circumstances were humble.

My mother would say, "If you can't have good friends, Johnny, do without. Don't be with people just to have people to be with." I didn't like that one, because as a boy my idea of a good friend didn't always agree with hers. Many times Mother knew instinctively which boys were good and which were bad. Her discernment, however, did not extend to the most important part of my life. She missed the fact that her son couldn't read.

THE OLD ADAGE that opposites attract was evident in our family. My father, Jack Waldon Corcoran, was the prototype of the gregarious, outgoing Irishman. He was born on a farm in North Dakota, his parents died when he was very young, and he and his younger brother Ken went to live with their grandmother. They were well provided for in a will, but their father's attorney, trustee of the estate, absconded with the money, leaving my father and his brother with nothing. The boys, however, not only were survivors, they were determined to make something of themselves. They earned scholarships to St. Thomas Academy in St. Paul, Minnesota, and graduated easily.

Father was a good student and won another scholarship, this time for football, to the University of St. Louis. He was only five-foot-ten, but solid and tough. He also loved to box, and his nose was broken so many times that part of one rib was grafted in to try to return his nose to its original shape. From then on he looked like Spencer Tracy who had gone 15 rounds with Jack Tunney.

He was a rough and tumble man, but gentle. Until the day he died I called him *Dada*, an affectionate Welsh or Irish name for "father." In later life, this childlike label frequently slipped into our adult conversation, to my embarrassment.

My father loved people, especially kids, and when he graduated, he went into teaching. As a member of the educational community, he was aware of the low pay, politics, and pitfalls, and he learned to maneuver through them. But he didn't like the game; he was a dreamer and an idealist. He used to say, "Johnny, there's some stuff going on out there that you just don't have to take. We have freedom in this country. In America, no one is *ever* really trapped. Remember that."

He never stayed at any one job long enough to be trapped. His work took him to 25 different neighborhoods in six states before I finished high school; I attended 17 different schools before I got my first full-time job. I've often wondered if he was fired each time or if he quit. Either way, he was the kind of man who would move on when the urge descended. Sometimes I wished he would allow himself to stay "trapped" for just a little longer, at least until I could make a good, lasting friend or two. But that never happened.

When I was in grade school I assumed the role of bodyguard for my five sisters. Marilyn, the oldest, was our little mother, because she was six when Patricia was born. I arrived only 15 months later. Marilyn wasn't too happy about a couple of new attention-grabbers moving into her territory; she didn't know three more would follow.

Eighteen months after me came Judy, who was a delight to tease. Nothing is more satisfying for a devilish older brother than having a vulnerable little sister to pick on. Judy was three and a half when Michele was born. We had been praying for a "Michael," but it didn't really matter, because once you were a Corcoran, you were loved. Two years later, Mama had Maureen, born during World War II. She was a very sick little girl and took a lot of Mother's attention. Times were hard, but we had one thing going for us through every trial — we had a tight-knit love.

WHEN AMERICA ENTERED World War II, we left Springfield, Illinois, where I attended kindergarten, and traveled to an army base in a foreign country: Texas. Father had been offered a job as director for the USO, but he had to go alone to New York for training. He put my pregnant mother and five children on the train for the trip to Abilene.

"Johnny," he said to me, "take care of your mother and sisters. And behave yourself." Dad waved good-bye with some apprehension, and rightly so.

A train ride during World War II meant soldiers and families, sad faces and nervous laughter; but to me it was pure adventure. I quickly took advantage of Mama's preoccupation with baby Michele and her own discomfort to venture into forbidden territory.

"Don't go between the cars, Johnny. Stay right near us," Mother admonished. But the risk and exhilaration of new experiences were too tempting. When Mama wasn't looking, I ventured out of our coach and rode on the swaying platform where the clickety-clack of the wheels was intensified and the soot left a film in my mouth. I pretended I was the sheriff pursuing robbers or imagined that out-laws were riding alongside, trying to leap onto the train while it was moving.

I pushed open the heavy doors between cars and visited the din-ing car, staring at the tables set with white tablecloths and silver in their proper places. Unfortunately, a conductor tapped me on the shoulder and said, "Go back to your mother, Sonny."

My reward for sitting still in my seat and looking quietly out the window was a bottle of pop, which I guzzled so fast that it came up before it went down. Mother said my accident was "divine inter-vention" because she didn't think she could have made it to Abilene without losing her mind if *something* hadn't slowed me down.

WHEN WE FINALLY arrived at the base, our promised housing wasn't available. The only thing we could find was an abandoned convent on the edge of town. There Mother was faced with another dilemma. On the convent grounds was a small church. Mother often told us, "Don't go into the church or you will not only have God to answer to, but I will report everything to your father." I wasn't sure who would inflict the worse punishment.

My sisters and I, however, had a field day. We were all over the little church, playing hide-and-seek on the altar and peeking out of the confessional. It was an intriguing place for our games, even though I imagined that the statues might open their tight lips and scold us for romping in sacred territory. Mother lived in constant fear that we might destroy some holy artifact and bring disgrace upon the family.

In Abilene I went to the first of three first-grade classrooms, and my father also introduced me to boxing. Since he was in charge of recreation for the servicemen, he thought a junior exhibition as a warm-up session before the Golden Gloves tournament might be entertaining. That would have been okay, except that I was supposed to be one of the contestants.

The dreaded day finally arrived. Another scrawny little kid, Paul Gene Smith, age eight, was pitted against Johnny Corcoran, age seven. Two or three hundred servicemen swarmed into the hall to watch these kids beat each other up. Paul and I were led, or perhaps pushed, into the ring, wearing boxing gloves that seemed twice as big as we were.

Once inside the ropes, I stood there facing Paul Gene, both of us wearing gargantuan mitts on our hands. *Maybe they'll fall off and we can get out of this.* With my arms dangling almost to the floor, I felt like one of the gorillas I'd seen in a Tarzan movie.

Paul Gene stared at me, and I stared right back. *He's a nice guy,* I thought. *Why are we fighting? I don't want to fight. Is it written somewhere that I need to be here?*

My father was giving me instructions. "Keep your right hand in front of your face. Lead with your left. You can do it, Johnny." *I can't even lift my arm. How can I keep it in front of my face?*

Jack Corcoran was my dad and I wanted to make him proud. If he said fight, I'd fight. But I hated it.

The servicemen clapped and hooted as we made jabs at each other. We danced around the ring like monkeys at the zoo. Finally, after what seemed like hours, the bell rang and the referee held up both our arms. "Johnny Corcoran and Paul Gene Smith are both winners," he called. The fight was declared a draw.

Years later I learned to fight hard and fight to win. When I didn't win, I developed the ability to convince myself that I had. Even with my face down in the mud, I clung to the idea that I was the winner. Nevertheless, fighting for any reason made me feel terrible.

In spite of the dreaded boxing ring, I loved the USOs, the soldiers who hoisted me on their shoulders, the smell of coffee, and the plates of sandwiches and cookies made by the ladies in the town.

Maureen, our family's fifth little girl, was born with severe asthma and had to remain in the hospital for several weeks. Mother stayed with her around the clock, leaving my father to cope with five children. That's when Marilyn, my oldest sister and second mother, who had reached her teens by this time, vanished one day without warning.

"Why did she leave, Dada?" I asked.

"I don't know, but we must find her," he told me. Mother and Father were frantic. They may have wondered if she had run off with a young soldier or if something even worse had happened. I remember how hurt I was that she had abandoned us, but in later years I understood something of her turmoil.

Marilyn had been an only child for six years, experiencing the stability of living in one place and having the attention of loving parents. Then changes occurred so rapidly that the once-secure little girl became like a billiard ball, struck from every direction and bounced from one side to the other. Move to a new place; a new sister is born; move again. We were living in a convent, bombarded by constant news reports about war: YANKS INVADE LEYTE ISLAND. NAZIS SURRENDER AT AACHEN. 5TH ARMY ADVANCES

IN ROME. A war we didn't understand consumed the adult conversation around us.

Because Mama's attention was focused on a sick baby, we children were left to fend for ourselves. Marilyn, an unhappy adolescent, was shoved in the background. She apparently was overcome with a growing desperation and decided to run away. Still, I felt she had violated our family code of loyalty.

Fortunately, we had known enough love that she didn't wander aimlessly, but instead escaped to the safety of our aunt's home in Chicago. After some anxious weeks, Marilyn did return home, but our lives were still in an upheaval.

And again the inevitable happened. Father came home one day and announced, "Agnes, we're going to Amarillo."

He had been so successful as a USO director in Abilene that my father was transferred to another base, us to another home, and me to another school. But even that was only for a time because before long we moved yet again to Roswell, New Mexico, and into a long, green military unit that housed four other families. For the third time in less than a year I entered a new first-grade classroom. I was the kid that no teacher had a chance to know.

"Johnny Corcoran? Oh, yes, he is the tall one, isn't he?" To my teachers I was just another body at a desk, too big to be invisible, too transient to be noticed. I never had the vaguest idea what first grade was about.

At the military bases, Mother became somewhat of a recluse. She was so immersed in her children, especially the baby, that she had no social life. She could not relate to the wives in our complex. "Those women have nothing to do but drink coffee and gab," she would say. And the pressures in her life were beginning to take their toll. I remember the day I went into the kitchen where she was ironing and I saw her crying.

It was April 1945, and the news had just come over the radio that President Franklin Roosevelt had died. The reports said, "Death, as the result of a cerebral hemorrhage, came painlessly to the 63-year-old president on the eve of his greatest triumphs — triumphs of the American armed forces he created to defend his country and a triumph of his plan for a new organization to keep the peace of the world."

Mother seemed very troubled, so I left her alone. When Father came home, I overheard her say something so shocking that I never forgot it. "Jack, this life is so hopeless. We might as well just turn on the gas."

I couldn't believe what my mother had said, and I was scared. I understood later that Roosevelt's death was only the proverbial straw that broke her spirit. All of the children, the constant moves, Maureen's illness, her isolation, and our unstable living conditions were affecting her deeply. She had lost hope in a stable, secure future. This was extremely disturbing to a small boy.

My mother, however, was a strong woman and also had a flare for drama. When her frustration was intense, the drama would come out. On only a few other occasions did I hear her suggest "the gas." But the impact of those moments influenced my behavior for years.

I must take care of Mama, I thought. *My dad can't always be here, so I have to be the man in the family.*

In order not to risk upsetting her, I began keeping things to myself that ordinarily a little boy might have shared with his mother. I became more secretive as the years went by. Because I didn't want to upset her, I never told her my fears or revealed my innermost thoughts.

After Roosevelt died, the world seemed to change so rapidly that every night the radio newscasters were broadcasting another startling announcement. Mussolini, the overstuffed, strutting dictator I had seen in the newsreels at the base theater, was killed. Just a couple of days later the man everybody hated, Adolf Hitler, committed suicide. Then the war in Europe was over and we were on the move again.

Father was excited. "I'll have a chance to teach again, something I've always loved," he said. "And we'll have a real house instead of army barracks," an idea that thrilled Mama and the girls.

"And Johnny," he said, "you can go to the same school where I'll be teaching." Now *that* really sounded good.

SANTA FE IN the late 1940s was a small town, rich in the history and tradition of Old Mexico, mixed with the trappings of 20th-century pioneers. Brick storefronts with neon signs and second-story ornamented window abutments surrounded a tree-filled town square bordered by electric gas lamps on iron columns. Prewar automobiles that all looked alike, with hump backs and tiny rear windows, parked in slanted rows on the streets. It looked wonderful to all of us after all those years in Army camps.

When we arrived we discovered our house wasn't ready and that we would have to call Chisholm Camp—a motor court on a dusty, unpaved street—our home.

Mother was distraught: "Imagine. A motor court! What do the Christian brothers think we are, truck drivers or construction workers? We were promised a real house!" Instead we found ourselves sleeping sideways on one bed and sharing the floor with a variety of Southwestern bugs.

I spent most of my time outside getting to know the construction workers and sensing their easy camaraderie, not unlike the soldiers

I had known at the bases. I was always on the go. (Today I probably would be diagnosed as having attention deficit disorder and given medication to calm me down.)

When we finally moved into an adobe house on one of the oldest streets in the Southwest, it was like living in American history books. Just a few paces from us was the oldest house in the United States, once the home of an Indian chief. The oldest government building in the country was there. Built in 1610, it was the past seat of authority under Spanish, Mexican, and American governments. On the corner was El San Miguel, more than 400 years old and the oldest church in the U.S. Conquistadors had ridden up and down the streets that were now my playground, and within walking distance were the courthouse, the governor's mansion, and the intriguing LaFonda Hotel.

My father made a nightly ritual of walking to the LaFonda. He would call out to anyone who was listening, "Who wants to go for a walk with me?" I would rush to grab his hand before one of my sisters beat me. I loved strolling down those historic streets with my dad, listening to his stories about Spanish explorers and Indian chiefs.

When we arrived at the LaFonda, he would buy some Roi-tan cigars, since they were the cheapest, and two newspapers, the *Denver Post* and the *Santa Fe New Mexican*. He had a smile and a greeting for almost everyone we met. "Hi, Ramon, how was your daughter's wedding?" "Jim, is your wife okay?" He had many friends, and I was always proud to be seen with him.

One night he said, "I'm going alone tonight, Johnny. You stay home with your sisters." I was very disappointed, but I trusted him and didn't argue. Then the idea hit me that my father shouldn't be going out by himself; I had no other choice but to follow him. It was dark and all the stores were closed, but I kept my resolve and didn't turn back. Finally, he reached the hotel, went in and bought his cigars and papers, and headed in the opposite direction from home. I crept out from behind a telephone pole where I was hiding and continued to shadow him. If I had suspected he needed protection before, I was sure of it then.

He walked several blocks, which seemed like miles to me, turned into somebody's front yard, went up on the porch, knocked on the door, and went in. I sneaked up to a window on the side of the house, stretched as high as I could, rested my chin on the sill, and peeked in. A number of men were sitting at a round table, smoking cigars, and dealing cards. After a while I saw them passing around red, white, and blue chips.

I thought, *I'm sure it's okay for my dad to play cards with his friends. He's safe. I'd better go.* But I was in trouble. There were no street lights, the moon was behind the clouds, and I didn't know how to get home. Minutes and hours went by; I paced back and forth, looked in the window, and paced some more. After what seemed like forever, I crawled into the backseat of a car that was sitting in the driveway and began to doze. I don't know how long it was before I heard a man call out, "Hey, Jack! There's a kid in my backseat and he looks like yours."

I became "unconscious." It's not easy to fake sleep while quivering inside, but somehow I pulled it off and my dad lifted me onto his lap while his friend drove us home. He carried me into the house, put me to bed, and never mentioned it again. I sensed that he knew I was not being defiant, but concerned. It's like having a puppy follow you to school. You know you should scold, but you realize he just wants to be with you, so you give him a hug instead.

WHEN CLASSES STARTED after Labor Day, I could hardly wait for the bell to ring. A school for boys sounded wonderful. Sisters were okay, but they didn't like to play rough. It took me only a few minutes to walk to St. Michael's, which stood on one corner of a large parcel of land envisioned by the brothers to become a college one day. An eight-foot wall surrounded the entire grounds, creating a fortress designed to either keep us in or keep the world out.

Seeing the corridor jammed with boys of all ages, boys with brown-skinned faces, black hair, and brown eyes, made me feel out of place. I looked different and talked differently but I liked the feeling. I ran up the steps, slowing down only when I reached a long hall where the brothers were waiting to welcome the students. I was shown to my second-grade class and said politely, as Mama had instructed, "Good morning, Brother." It looked a lot better than my three first-grade rooms. So I smiled at the teacher and sat down at a desk near the front.

And there, in that big red brick building within the tall stone walls, I began a 40-year battle inside my own private prison.

You are a complex tapestry, woven with a million strands,
some of which reach back to Adam and beyond him to God
who created you in His image. But many of the most important
threads in the complex design of who you are were introduced
in your childhood.
— David Seamands, *Putting Away Childish Things*

CHAPTER 3

Johnny the Innocent

J OHNNY CORCORAN, STEP UP HERE. Quickly, now." I could feel
40 pairs of eyes burrowing into my back. From my seat to Brother
Abdon's desk seemed like a painful mile and a half. At St. Michael's
School for Boys in Santa Fe, walking that gauntlet was more humiliating than throwing up. *What have I done to deserve demerits?*

There were seven rows of old-fashioned hardwood school desks
in our class — the kind with attached wooden seats and metal legs.
I sat in row seven, in the very last seat at the back of the room, the
place they called the dumb row. *Why was I there?*

Brother Abdon, a handsome young second-grade teacher who
looked as if he didn't need a razor, stood behind his desk in his long
black cassock and skull cap, tapped a yardstick on the floor, and
motioned me to walk faster. My feet felt like I was wading through
sand with my boots on.

"Two demerits, Johnny," intoned Brother Abdon. "One for not completing the sentences in your workbook and one for refusing to read the letters on the blackboard. Roll up your pant legs."

I THOUGHT BROTHER Abdon was my friend. At recess he encouraged my athletic ability and cheered when I won. *Why did he punish me in the classroom?*

Standing in front of row seven, I could see every kid who walked up the aisle. The brother handed the yardstick to each boy, who took careful aim and swatted me on my calves. If they gave me a stinging blow, I would glare with my best I'll Get You Outside look. If I got just a light tap, Brother Abdon would take the stick and issue a resounding whack on my benefactor's backside. It was a no-win situation.

When I finally slid into my seat, I avoided the brother's eyes and opened my reader, staring down at those weird lines that marched across the page like snowflakes, every one uniquely different. They seemed to melt before they made sense.

Nothing was wrong with my eyesight. I could pick out the most remote star on a clear New Mexico night or thread my mother's smallest needle. When I looked above the blackboard that lined the two walls of our schoolroom, I could see every detail on the portraits of 32 United States presidents who stared down at me. But those gigantic ABCs were from another planet.

In the second grade we were expected to recite the alphabet. But I couldn't do the ABCs — not until the sixth grade when I learned the alphabet song, and even then I only recited the letters from memory.

"Johnny, let's try again," Brother Abdon persisted. "A...B...C," he said slowly and then pointed at me. The idea was for a student to jump up and say "D-E-F," and then that student would point to someone else who'd say "G-H-I," and so on.

"Now, you tell me the next three letters, Johnny."

Couldn't he see I was invisible?

"Johnny, what are the next three letters? Speak up, now."

Here comes another demerit. It was easier to be quiet, lower my eyes, and pretend I wasn't there. Brother Abdon would tell me to "try harder," but I didn't know what I was supposed to try harder to do.

I looked down at my inkwell, wishing I could shrink so small that I could jump in and hide. But it was impossible for me to go unnoticed. My classmates were mostly boys from middle-class or wealthy Spanish and Mexican families, many of them boarders who lived in dormitories. The big, blond Irish kid who sat in the Dumb Row, along with a few children from Mexico who couldn't speak a word of English, was as conspicuous as a marshmallow floating in a cup of cocoa.

It didn't occur to me in the second grade, or in the third, that my seat at the back of the room, the demerits and punishment, all were related to my inability to read. I was like an American tourist trying to decipher the street signs or read a newspaper in Tokyo. Nothing made sense. I could understand numbers, but when the reading began I was in a foreign country. And the swats didn't hurt nearly as much as the humiliation.

R-r-r-ring! Saved by the bell again! We lined up like little soldiers, marched to freedom, and broke ranks with whoops and hollers when we hit the playground. That was my turf and recess was my salvation. Inside, no one would choose me for a spelling team; outside, I was king of the mountain.

The brothers would organize games and tell us to choose our teams. "Come on, guys, let's play horse," I yelled, imitating my father's commanding voice. He was the athletic coach at St. Michael's, which didn't buy me fame and fortune with the teachers inside, but gave me a certain degree of respect outside.

"Horse" was like medieval jousting from a child's perspective. One kid would ride on another's shoulders and try to pull the opposing riders off until only one person remained on his horse. I chose Juan as my rider, for two reasons: He was the smartest kid in the class and sat in row one, but he was also the smallest and least athletic. He was usually left out of team selection until the last. We were opposites who bonded.

Juan and I were an unbeatable pair and everyone knew it, including Brother Abdon. With my size and his agility we charged and retreated, maneuvering like a star quarterback running 70 yards for a touchdown.

Inevitably the bell would ring again and we would have 45 seconds to line up to go back to class. The winners could stand in front of the line, so Juan and I took our places ahead of the others. I knew what it was like to be first, and I knew what it was like to be last.

I wished Juan would teach me those ABCs and how they fit into a book. *Maybe learning to read is something you just catch someday,* I reasoned, *like the measles.*

One tactic I used to boost my attitude was singing a little ditty from the movie *Song of the South* called "Zip-a-dee-doo-dah." That happy little tune became my theme song. Sometimes when things really got tough, I just put my head down on the desk and hummed the tune. It helped.

SINCE MY FATHER was the coach, I spent a lot of time with the guys on the football team. They were like big brothers and a welcome reprieve from five sisters at home. I was proud when I was asked to be the water boy, a job I took very seriously. I was certain that if I didn't run on the field with my milk bottles filled with water, the players would faint and not be able to finish the game. And if they lost, it would be all my fault.

This is my chance to show I'm important to the school. Who cares if I'm in the dumb row, just as long as I take care of the team.

My opportunity for fame came during the game of the year between St. Michael's and its arch rival, Santa Fe High. It was a close contest, so I was very excited when the first quarter ended and it was my turn to shine. I grabbed my little metal carrier containing eight one-quart glass milk bottles filled with cool water and bounded onto the field to revive the parched throats of my big brothers.

Everyone was watching me.

But my moment of triumph suddenly turned to disaster when I tripped and fell flat on my face, shattering all eight bottles and showering the turf with shards of broken glass. I was humiliated beyond endurance. So rather than facing the disgrace of having to look at anyone, I chose to pass out.

I played the role to the hilt, keeping my eyes closed and remaining limp as I was carried off the field on a stretcher. The team trainer hovered over me and my father ran to see if I was hurt. Just as the second half began, I conveniently regained consciousness, but held my breath for the rest of the game, fearing that someone might get sliced by a piece of glass that hadn't been removed.

I certainly wasn't a hero, but I had learned how to avoid an uncomfortable situation by indulging in a little play acting. No one would know the difference.

What would Dada think? He had been so proud of me and I had let him down. But I saw the look in his eyes when he was told that I hadn't been injured and I knew that he loved *me*, not what I did. That kind of love, coupled with the awareness that I had caused my parents troubled moments, made me feel very guilty — but not enough to tell them the truth. They trusted me implicitly, and because of my classroom inadequacy, I wanted to be perfect in every other area of my life. I had to be like Superman, ever on guard that some Kryptonite would not expose the real me.

Somewhere in the second or third grade I began to understand that it wasn't just the way I looked that made me different. I knew I would never amount to anything if I didn't get out of the dumb row.

Brother Abdon never came to me and said, "Johnny, I know you can't read. Let me help you." With due respect to the good brother, learning deficiencies (or disabilities) were not understood in the 1940s.

Why didn't my book-loving parents know what was happening to me as I slumped in the dumb row? When my report card came home they must have been shocked. A row of F's right down the line, except for arithmetic. If they went to my teachers, and I believe they did, they probably heard the same explanation so many parents have heard:

"Mrs. Corcoran, your son is a smart boy. Don't worry about him; he'll catch up in time."

"Coach, Johnny is growing so fast that it will take time for his mind to match his body."

Most likely, they received this advice, familiar and frustrating to parents everywhere: "Mr. and Mrs. Corcoran, we are teachers who have been trained to teach your children. Don't try to teach Johnny yourselves; leave it to us."

Myths and denials were woven into excuses for not teaching every child to read. This wasn't intentional or mean-spirited; they simply didn't have any idea why Johnny, and many others like me, couldn't read.

During my two years at St. Michael's I began to acquire a lifelong library. My books consisted not of words on paper, but of observations and experiences. My curricula was not English grammar or literature — those were foreign subjects — but the study of people from every age, background, and color. Those "books" were my educational tools. Some I kept on permanent file in my memory box; others I learned to use or discard for my own purposes.

One of my good "books" was Brother Ignatius. Mama would invite him for dinner and work her magic at stretching a meal. The invitation was a real tribute to him, considering that we scarcely had enough money to feed and clothe all eight of us. He returned the favor by dropping in frequently with food. And after dinner, Brother Iggie would play ball with us. "You're a natural athlete, Johnny," he would tell me. He really knew the way into a young boy's heart.

Brother Alfred, the school administrator, was another brother who befriended the family by stopping in with a bag of groceries or some clothing. In the years after the war, there were shortages of many things, and it was not unusual for people to share with one another. Since we were often very short of money, we appreciated his generosity. One of my sisters would see him coming and call, "Here comes Brother Alfred," and we would scramble to the door to see what bounty he had brought. He worked in the school office and had a big set of keys hanging on a sash around his waist so that he jingled when he walked. I thought he must be a very important person.

One evening he came by with some fresh vegetables from his garden and suggested what sounded like an exciting escapade. He had access to all the rooms in the school, so his plan was simple, yet daring.

"We'll pretend we're Robin Hood's merry men and raid the student store. We'll make believe we are going to rob the rich to give to the poor," Brother Alfred said in a conspiratorial voice. "Who would like to join me in Sherwood Forest?"

Three voices echoed, "I would!" "Can I go?" "Me too!"

"Fine," said Brother Alfred, "but we won't tell your mother and father until we return with our treasures. This will be our secret."

Patricia, Judy, and I quickly got into the spirit of the game. The student store had all of the candy, cookies, and soft drinks we couldn't afford. I was sure Brother Alfred was going to treat us, because, after all, he wouldn't do anything wrong.

When he unlocked the door to the room full of riches, he whispered, "Don't turn on the lights. We don't want the King's henchman to discover us."

I didn't know much about the story of Robin Hood, but I had an imagination and loved adventure. Young as we were, however, we suddenly knew that Brother Alfred was different. I was almost eight and had been around soldiers when my father was in charge of the USO in Abilene. I had sharp ears and overheard a lot of things I wouldn't have told my parents. I wasn't dumb about some things. And I sensed this brother wasn't the good man he pretended to be.

Patricia was nine years old and in the fourth grade; Judy was in second. I was right in the middle and very protective of my sisters. I placed myself between Brother Alfred and the girls as we weaved in and out of the candy counters, stuffing our pockets with Hershey bars and gumdrops. After all, candy was candy. But every time I heard those keys jingle near us, I'd push Patricia and Judy out of the way as the brother tried to reach out and touch them. Brother Alfred didn't seem to like it that I could outwit him, but I wasn't going to let him get near my sisters. I wasn't afraid, just angry that we had been tricked.

"Come on, kids, let's go," the brother finally muttered. He didn't sound like the same person who came to our house with presents. My sisters scrambled for the door, and I followed, acting as a buffer between them and Brother Alfred. The girls were scared, but they weren't exactly sure why.

Brother Alfred had the right bait, and with his Roman collar he thought he had the right camouflage. The sad part is that we trusted him until we were alone with him; but then our trust vanished. We never mentioned it to our parents, but we sneaked into the student store once more, continuing to play duck and dodge with the brother. He never won the game, and after a while he stopped coming around.

Both Brother Iggie and Brother Alfred represented the Church to me and became a part of my good and evil library books. To me they were as different as Christ and Hitler. Even in third grade I began to understand that my trust and faith could not be built on individuals, but only on my family and on God.

I could read people. I knew I wasn't dumb. *So why did they keep me in the dumb row?*

One million American children between the ages
of 12 and 17 cannot read above the third-grade level.
—National Institute for Literacy, 1992

CHAPTER 4

Survival Game

N EXT STOP, LOS ALAMOS, New Mexico," Dada announced as Ernie, our 1937 Dodge, chugged up to the guard station where we stopped to show our identification. We had driven up the winding road from the valley of the Rio Grande along the face of the Jemez mountains until we came to The Hill, which is what the natives called Los Alamos. I stared at the high fence and the security service guards in trooper hats and gray-blue uniforms who were manning the gate. Looking up, I could see a tower with more guards, and beyond that loomed two tanks. That was scary.

An armed guard poked his head into the car, unmoved by the children crammed and wiggling in the seats, and asked for our credentials. Father showed a pass that proved he had a job as coach and recreational director in this remote place, and we were waved through the gates. This was better than Orphan Annie's secret decoder ring.

After the war, Los Alamos was a crowded, dusty, clamoring little community, plumped down like an afterthought on a remote and beautiful mountainside. It was the site of the Manhattan Project, headed by Dr. J. R. Oppenheimer and staffed by a team of scientists and technicians who developed the atomic bomb, which had changed the course of human history. Top-secret research was still being conducted, and the growing civilian population was challenging community planners. It was a place where the average age was about 30 and the population, which was close to 9,000, included 1,300 children. What a place for an adventurous kid!

I DIDN'T CARE that a Quonset hut or house identical to hundreds of others would be our home. It didn't matter to me that sidewalks were nonexistent and streets unpaved, but it would upset Mama. The most important thing for me was a new school. I had escaped from St. Michael's and the dumb row.

Would someone teach me how to read? Would someone see that I wasn't dumb and give me the magic that would make sense out of those words in books?

The school at Los Alamos was born out of necessity and without careful planning. When the wives of the atomic scientists arrived at the site, they didn't know what their husbands were doing, nor did they realize there was no school for their children. So they took the initiative to start a one-room school. As the population increased, a professional educator was brought in who had the drab classrooms repainted and added music, art, and many other courses. By the time we arrived, the enrollment had grown to 600 children and was increasing rapidly.

On my first day of fourth grade, I learned two things. First, there were girls in the school; and second, the teacher and the children sat in a semicircle, with one of the students acting as chairman of the classroom discussion. *Oh, boy, no dumb row.* When I was older, I realized this was my introduction to progressive education.

This is great. I won't sit in the back of the room. No swats. And girls aren't so bad.

I sang "Zip-a-dee-doo-dah," my own special theme song, all the way home. I might not have a bluebird sitting on my shoulder, but I was just sure everything was going to be just fine.

Then I received another surprise in my educational journey: My fourth-grade class had reading groups. Redbirds. Bluebirds. Buzzards. The latter were the nonreaders. What was I? A Buzzard! Could I get any lower?

There was one saving grace, and her name was Heidi. She was one of the smartest kids in school, and the fact that she had beautiful blond curls heightened my preadolescent interest. (I was always attracted to the brightest girls, and if most of them were pretty, that was an added bonus.)

Heidi was in the top reading circle, so I wanted to be there too. I knew my multiplication tables and had learned all the Roman numerals up to one hundred in Catholic school. But neither of those accomplishments could make me a Bluebird or Redbird. I had seen buzzards circling dead animals in the desert, and they made me sick.

My mind was continually whirling with new games to play at recess to show off my physical ability. When we played chase games on the playground, I always wanted to tag Heidi, but I was afraid that if I caught her (which I could easily have done), she would ignore me because I was a Buzzard. So I didn't try.

I was also introduced to a new method of punishment in fourth grade. I wasn't sure which was worse — the swats with the yardstick back at St. Michael's or the silence in Los Alamos. One teacher tried to cure me by saying, "Johnny, read the first sentence on page two," and then allowing minutes to pass until I thought I would burn up and disintegrate in front of the entire class.

"Johnny," she would say, "has the cat got your tongue?"

I never understood that question because it seemed so stupid. But then, the teacher thought that I was stupid too. I would stare at the book, able only to read the number at the top of the page. The rest of the lines hadn't changed since my third-grade reader. When it became evident that I wasn't going to speak, she would let out a slight sigh and pass on to the next student.

I became a nonperson, acting like I didn't care, but beginning to evaluate the educational haves and have-nots. I was a nothing.

ONE SPRING DAY, after I was convinced that I would always be different from everyone else, I heard the siren call of baseball. I raced out of class at 3:00 P.M., yearning for someplace where I could prove that I wasn't the boy who sat mutely in school, but a home-run hitter, a budding candidate for the Baseball Hall of Fame.

Only the seventh and eighth graders played on the school team, but I grabbed my glove anyway and raced toward the ball field. I was almost as tall as the older boys, so no one paid much attention to me as I stood behind the batting cage watching the game with burning desire. Neither team wore uniforms and there was no outfield fence, but this was the major leagues to me.

A big kid on the opposing team had already belted the ball over the right fielder's head during his first two times up. Then there were two outs, the bases were loaded, and the big kid was at the plate again.

Run out deep into right field, I said to myself. Just as I did—*crack!*—the ball was spinning across the sky, and our guys were running all over the field. Suddenly, I had it! The ball was snug inside the glove on my left hand and I heard those beautiful words from the umpire: "You're out!"

Our team raced toward the bench, and I joined in as if I belonged. My heart was thumping with excitement. *They have to let me in the game now*, I thought. *Either that, or the manager will get mad and send me home.*

"Hey, you — Blondie," someone yelled at me, "you bat third this inning."

I am in, I am in! Now I can be somebody, not just a silent Buzzard.

When it was my turn, I walked to the plate in a trance. Three fast balls whizzed by me. I couldn't even connect. "Strike three!" roared the umpire. I was out.

For the next 38 years I was the boy who infiltrated the game, played the part of the winner, only to arrive at a moment of truth when my inadequacies were revealed. On one hand I was an overachiever; but on the other, I always felt I was falling short.

OUTSIDE OF SCHOOL, Los Alamos was a place of mystery and intrigue. I listened to the stories my father would tell about the secret experiments and startling events that had been revealed by President Harry Truman. I was told how the president and an important man by the name of Churchill had given Japan a chance to surrender, but the offer was refused. Then two cities with strange names, Hiroshima and Nagasaki, were hit with enormous bombs and Japan decided to give up after all.

Los Alamos had exciting places for young boys to explore. My new friend Wilbur, my dog Boogie, and I would take every opportunity to investigate forbidden territory.

We would head out after school with candy bars to sustain us in our search and walk to the open areas on the edge of town. We were Jack Armstrong, the All-American Boy, Superman, and the Lone Ranger all in one.

"Wilbur, what does that say?" I pointed to a sign in front of a wire fence.

"It says DANGER...CON-TAM-IN-A-TED AREA," Wilbur answered, stumbling over the longer word neither one of us knew.

"Sounds like fun," I said with small boy bravado. "Let's go."

Wilbur, Boogie (my mutt couldn't read, either), and I would scramble over or under the fence and find wonderful treasures — a piece of metal, canteens, C rations, and other booty that we could stuff in our pockets to trade or hoard. Most of our loot, however, we didn't dare take home. Instead we would play war games for hours.

One day, as we trooped through forbidden land, we saw another big sign with a skull and crossbones on it, just like some of Mama's cleaning stuff. "What's that, Wilbur?" I asked, looking at the strange markings.

"KEEP OUT — RESTRICTED," he deciphered.

That was like saying sic 'em to a dog. "Let's go, guys," I commanded, and Wilbur, Boogie, and I were off again to find more booty.

We were pirates, enemy soldiers, Indian scouts. Best of all, Wilbur could read and I could use him, as I did all my literate friends, to further my education. Surely God protected two mischievous boys and their dog from potentially lethal substances that may have been lingering in those forbidden fields.

THE MOVIES WERE another important part of our recreation. Wilbur and I took pride in sneaking Boogie into the show with us. He was well behaved and only became excited when we would whoop and holler with Roy Rogers or Hopalong Cassidy. My sisters would sometimes come along, and although most of the audience were military, there was never any concern about us going unchaperoned. All the serials ended with "To Be Continued Next Week," and we couldn't wait for the next episode. It was serious business, after all, to find out how the hero escaped from the bandits who had trapped him on top of a train headed for a tunnel. We *had* to go back next Saturday. I also learned from the newsreels — Paramount News — the eyes and ears of the world — and amazed Dada that I could carry on a conversation about current events.

When we first arrived, movie admission was ten cents, but one day we were told that a new War Department regulation increased the price to 15 cents for children. I knew I had to earn more money to pay for my recreational pleasures. Entrepreneurial fever hit me.

I heard that some of the bigger kids sold newspapers, and so I knew that if I wanted a piece of the action I had to outsmart them with new techniques. I bought the papers for three cents from a high school kid who was a distributor, then sold them for five cents. At first I didn't have the capital to finance this enterprise, so I bought some stock on credit from a friend of mine (who acted as middleman) until I had accumulated enough pennies to buy my own papers. That was high finance.

After the war, construction boomed in Los Alamos. The building projects that had been on hold while America was making an all-out defense effort were brought out of mothballs. When the workers left The Hill after work, long lines of cars would drive down through the guard gate at the bottom. Since carpooling was demanded, every car was full.

Newspaper territories were staked out by the biggest and toughest kids, and I didn't like that. Between 3:30 and 4 P.M. I would station myself near the gate, where the cars had to slow down or stop before proceeding. I would find the end of the line and wave my papers at the cars, putting on my biggest smile. I'd sell anywhere from two to five papers to the occupants of each car and would hesitate just long enough to get a tip. My goal was to sell 50 papers a day. At a time when a candy bar was a nickel, a dollar was a fortune.

ONE DAY MY "rich" Aunt Dorothy and her family came to visit us. My mother was very excited about the visit, but I panicked. I had heard so much about my brilliant cousins who were always at the top of their classes. When they arrived, I sneaked out back and crunched into Boogie's dog house.

This wasn't an adventure; it was pure torture. I hid until it was almost dark and Mama was calling me for supper. *If I hide long enough, there won't be enough time to talk about school. It will be just too humiliating for them to find out I can't read.*

Somehow, I managed to avoid any conversations about my lack of scholarship.

I LOVED SUNDAYS at Los Alamos when Dada would pile us into Ernie after church and drive down from The Hill to visit the Hopi villages. He would tell us stories about the Indian history and culture; he believed they had been mistreated, and this influenced my own opinions. I never understood why Indians were always the bad guys in the movies.

We stayed in Los Alamos for more than a year, which was plenty of time to learn to read. But when we left, although I had gained new knowledge in history, mathematics, business, geography, and sociology, the contents of a book were still an utter mystery to me.

IT WAS INEVITABLE we would move again. Father had a better job offer, so the nomadic Corcorans packed and headed back to Santa Fe, into a big house infested with mice.

When school started, I was in the fifth grade. The teachers had passed me once more. They had labels for kids like me.

"Not motivated." *But I want desperately to read.*

"Johnny is very immature." *What am I supposed to be?*

"Won't respond to class work." *It is easier to be silent.*

I entered Carlos Gilbert School in Santa Fe with the same sense of anticipation with which I had greeted every new class and teacher before. This time, however, it was a different educational experience. This was a real war zone.

In fifth grade I learned to fight for my rights. I was a minority Anglo in a school that was 75 percent Hispanic. The first observation I made was that the Mexican boys seemed more mature than the Anglos. Some of them knew the tricks of extortion and intimidation, and they used them on me.

My prized red bicycle had to stay locked in my house because I soon found out it would not be safe at Carlos Gilbert. And I began to pace myself so that I arrived at school exactly when the bell rang. I tried to avoid the battleground outside the building, but during recess there was no place to hide.

I quickly learned that if I tried to defend myself against a kid who hit me, I would soon have a gang descend and give me a good beating. I also found some allies who stood up for me when the chips were down: two girls who sat in the new dumb row with me.

Judging by certain signs of maturity my experienced 11-year-old eyes observed, Dolores and Maria were older than most of the fifth graders. On more than one occasion, they intervened on my behalf in the cafeteria, in the hall, and on the playground.

"Hey, you, Gringo, get outta my way," one of the guys, supported by two or three others, would shout as he gave me a shove. I wanted to stay out of trouble, especially when I was outnumbered. But Dolores and Maria, who were bigger and bolder than the boys, would stand in front of me and shout, "Deja le solo," with the same authority I had heard from my older sisters when they issued me a dare-not-disobey order. The Mexican boys would retreat for a time, and I would have a short reprieve.

I really don't know why those two girls wanted to be my protectors. Perhaps it was because we shared the dumb row together. Whatever their reasons, they were important "books" in my library, found under the card file labeled "good Samaritans." Their kind deeds uprooted the seeds of prejudice and bigotry that otherwise might have germinated in my young mind.

One day when Dolores and Maria weren't around, a kid who wanted to prove his toughness in order to be accepted as part of a gang kicked me so hard I felt the pain all day. I ignored him because the gang was waiting to attack if I began to fight. I wanted to live without getting beat up.

Just learn how to survive, Johnny.

A few days later, I caught my tormentor standing at the urinal. So I walked up behind him, grabbed him by the neck and squeezed as hard as I could. "If you ever kick me again, I'll put your head down the toilet," I said in my most villainous voice. He zipped up his pants and ran out of the bathroom. After he left, I was one scared kid.

A short time later, I was walking home from school when another gang member gave me a taste of the hit-and-run routine. Enraged, I chased him down the block and gave him an unmerciful beating. Evidently the word traveled fast because half the school had followed him to watch the confrontation. When my victim was down for the count, I picked him up and stuffed him in a trash can.

The next day there was cautious respect for me on the playground, along with a new name. They called me loco because of the garbage can incident. I realized this was a new disguise I could use. If I acted crazy, the gang wouldn't know how I would respond, and they would leave me alone. So I walked around with my eyes staring, my mouth hanging open, and my body jerking in wild contortions. It worked — but I knew it wasn't really me.

I didn't have many friends at school, except for Dolores and Maria, unless you counted Mrs. Romero. She was the only teacher who acknowledged that I had a reading deficiency. One day she said, "Johnny, if you mow my lawn, I'll help you with your reading."

I cut her grass, but she never taught me to read.

HOW DID I pass from grade to grade? How did I remain in the back of the room or in the Buzzard circle with no one coming to my aid? Is there a place or a person to blame?

Parents of children who can't read either deny the problem or believe it will eventually be solved. Teachers who have been trained in certain methods can't or won't adapt their system to an individual child. Ultimately, the students themselves are blamed.

Many people have rationalized, "He didn't learn to read because he moved so many times." That certainly might have been a contributing factor, but how long does it take to teach a child the alphabet or to sound out words phonetically? Is a year enough? Two years?

I stayed in many schools for a year or more. How do you explain the children of military personnel who often move as much as I did but still learned to read. No, it wasn't frequent moves, crowded class-rooms, other languages being spoken, or overworked teachers. It was because no one took it upon himself or herself to teach me.

So every year I became more resourceful in dealing with the pain at school, in disguising what I thought was a permanent defect. I became the boy with the mask, hiding my scars like the Phantom of the Opera.

Only God could have known how abandoned I felt.

*School year followed school year and the children got
unhappier and unhappier, ridiculed, called 'dumb' by
schoolmates, isolated, punished for they knew not what crimes.*
— Rudolf Flesch, *Why Johnny Still Can't Read*

CHAPTER 5

Idiot Masquerade

EACH YEAR I PASSED FROM grade to grade, like a boy in a revolving door. I was moving, but no one showed me how to step out into the mainstream with kids who could read.

When we moved to Albuquerque, I entered sixth grade by turning in my badge of innocence and becoming a rebel against school authorities. I looked upon teachers as my oppressors, real or imagined. *If they won't treat me right, if they make me feel dumb, I'll get even somehow.*

It was as true in 1953 as it is today: If a child doesn't learn to read by the time he's in fifth grade, his chances of remaining illiterate are greatly increased. Nonreaders (illiterate boys, especially) disrupt the classroom, fade into the background, get sick, or ask to go to the bathroom when it is their turn to read. Most teachers (especially male teachers) will let girls go to the restroom without question. Ultimately children who can read are affected by those who can't, and everyone loses in the process.

Dad was athletic coach at the Indian school in Albuquerque, a grinning Irishman in sharp contrast to kids from Navajo, Laguna, Acoma, Zuni, Hopi, and Apache tribes. But he loved his young athletes, and they responded with winning teams.

The campus included farms, dairy cows, pigs, sheep, chickens, and ducks, so farming was an important part of my informal schooling. A 12-year-old Navajo boy taught me that sheep were more than just Mary's little lamb. The Native Americans I added to my library of "books" were not like the ones I saw in the movies. They were quiet, noncompetitive, and loved crafting belts, watchbands, and carvings. I remember running races with my Indian friends; their idea of winning was to reach the finish line at the same time. When we played basketball it was like a silent movie — all motion, no talking.

During our Sunday drives to the various pueblos north of Santa Fe, my parents taught us respect for the Indians. Native American culture and tribal dances fascinated me. I was getting an education, but by the standards of literate society, I was a dumb kid, a slow learner, a trouble maker.

OUR HOUSE WAS right on the campus of the Indian school and was the haven I needed when I entered another wing of hell called North 4th Street School. When I left home each day it was like jumping from a comfortable warm shower into icy water without taking time to dry off. Home and the Indian school were safe harbors, full of treasures I cherish to this day. School, on the other hand, was my first battle with authority and a more brutal form of discrimination.

North 4th Street was a predominantly Mexican school, with only about six Anglo athletes. I quickly sized up the situation and knew that I needed to make friends with the right people. Skinny was one of the toughest kids in school, so I began to cultivate him. He could neutralize the tough Mexican kids, and I needed that ally.

THEN THERE WAS Leroy. He was the brain and was even bigger than me. Nobody, but nobody, picked on Leroy. I needed him on my side too.

We were the terrible trio, disrupting the class with our antics and wisecracks. From a compliant little Irish Catholic, faithfully going to confession, I began to develop a dual personality: obedient son at home, wise guy in school. It was an introduction to the many years of masquerading that followed.

One day I was told I would be transferred to Mrs. Richardson's room from a class taught by a man who had no control over us. Mrs. Richardson was a no-nonsense woman. She didn't need to look at me when she said, "Any shenanigans out of you and the punishment will be detention after school and a note to your parents." I knew whom she meant. Staying after school was the worst punishment she could give a kid who hated school as much as I did. But when I did stay, Mrs. Richardson would help me with my penmanship, even though the letters didn't make sense. I adored her from the first day, and the fact that she was young and pretty didn't have anything to do with my infatuation.

Maybe school won't be so bad after all.

She discovered very quickly that I couldn't read or spell and had a hard time coping with schoolwork. "Johnny, why don't you try harder?" she would ask, melting my young heart with her beautiful eyes. I couldn't answer.

Try harder, try harder. Why do teachers tell me to try harder? Try doing what?

She was one of the best math and penmanship teachers I had, and certainly the finest disciplinarian; but she also failed to teach me to read, passing me on to the next grade just like all the others had done.

Mrs. Richardson, why didn't you teach me to read? Why didn't you try harder?

Today teachers come to me and ask, "Why didn't you tell your teachers you wanted help?" I was a child who really didn't know the question to ask and isn't it the responsibility of the teacher to know if the student has a reading deficiency and to provide the proper instruction? I was led to believe that it was *my* fault I couldn't read.

How did I compensate? I found my outlet in athletics. I was tall and fast, and with my father as coach and mentor, I became a star on the court, acquiring a skill that took me through many tight spots in the years to come. I began to develop confidence in my survival tactics: Continue to cultivate the smartest and toughest kids, develop my athletic talents, and pose as an idiot when expedient.

"Hey, Johnny, can't you read? The sign says Teacher's Lounge."

I would open my mouth, give a blank stare, and turn on my stupid act. "Duh, wassa matta? Don ya' think I know it?" I could scratch my head and shuffle my feet to play the part of the village moron. I was the class clown who hid his shame behind a false face.

When the Indian school closed for the summer, Dad went to a nearby town to take a job, and Mother went to work in a drugstore. She left every afternoon at 3 P.M. and didn't come home until late at night. New responsibilities fell on my shoulders.

"Johnny, you're in charge now. Be sure you stay near the house to play. Call me if you need me." Like other working mothers, she would dash off, leaving me to assume the role of father while she was at the drugstore and Dad was working at any job he could get during school vacation. Patricia and I became the chief authorities at home when my oldest sister married. I had wanted to be a leader, and finally I had my chance.

IN SEVENTH GRADE it was back to Catholic school again, where I knew the line of authority. But now I felt like I was living in a strange world and didn't know the language. I knew its rules, but I couldn't follow them. *Why can't they see I'm just as smart as that kid who has his hand up all the time?*

At St. Theresa's I had a temporary triumph. I tried out for the crossing patrol and was accepted. I put on the red jacket and white belt and, as a member of a four-man platoon under the training of the city police, rose to the rank of lieutenant in charge. I was very proud of my position because I was demonstrating to the police and to the school that I had leadership qualities.

But one day I received a notice to turn in my jacket and belt. I was dismissed from the patrol because my academics were poor. "Johnny just isn't working hard enough in class" was the explanation. I was so hurt that I didn't tell my parents I had been kicked off of my important job. The nuns had betrayed me and had stripped me of my sense of worth. It was the first time my performance in the classroom had affected my outside activities, and the blow left me as deflated as a balloon without air. I was especially angry with those who had flattened me.

Junior high was no longer a game — it was a battlefield. It was me against the literate world. Fed up with parochial school, I said to my parents, "I would really like to go to public school. It would save money for you, and, besides, it's a lot nearer home."

Mother and Father were convinced this might be a good move, so I was allowed to check in late at Jefferson Junior High.

I felt like I was in a maze at a carnival, only this wasn't fun. I had six 45-minute classes, six teachers, and a list of classrooms I couldn't find. I didn't have any friends and I couldn't read the schedule or figure out what door to open, so I simply didn't go to school. I was treacherously close to becoming another statistic among dropouts when I met an unlikely mentor.

Vince was a 17-year-old Mexican kid who could barely speak English and was a "graduate" of Juvenile Hall, having served time for stealing a Harley-Davidson. He wasn't exactly the kind of friend my parents would have chosen.

Vince and I were the same height, even though he was four years older. He had long, thick, black hair, slick with pomade and combed in a duck tail. He wore a thin, black leather belt with his pegged khaki pants low on his hips. He made scraping sounds as he walked in his spit-shined cordovan leather shoes with thick soles and taps on the heels. He had a small cross tattooed on his hand between his thumb and forefinger, the sign of his particular gang.

His pals called him Pachuco, a Mexican expression for an outlaw that evolved to a greeting among gang members. We were an odd couple.

"Come on, Gringo, I'll show you where I work," Vince said, so I went with him to the bowling alley. I lied about my age and got a job as a pin boy. Vince taught me how to pick up four pins at a time, two in each hand. This was an important skill to know. I learned some great lessons from my new friend. Some of them were even good.

"Listen to me, Gringo," Vince said to me one day. "Juvenile Hall ain't no place to be. It's hell. They take away your own duds and make you wear a uniform. If I'd stayed in school I probably wouldn't have gone to jail."

I respected his advice, though I don't know why — maybe because he was almost 18 and knew his way around.

"You go back to school, Gringo. The bowling alley ain't no place for a kid like you."

When Vince invited me to his house in Old Town, I was afraid to go to the barrio. It was on the southeast side of Albuquerque where the kids who lived in The Heights were warned not to go. But his mother welcomed me with a big hug and invited me to stay and eat. I stayed. In this case even my parents would probably have agreed with my staying. It would have been impolite to do anything else. She cooked on a wood-burning stove, aromatic with pinewood, and flipped tortillas directly on the iron top. Filled with spicy beans, those tortillas filled my stomach, while her acceptance captured my heart.

These people are just like us. They aren't outlaws.

Through Vince I learned again that race, color, and creed have nothing to do with an individual's worth. He unknowingly erased my prejudices and inspired me to continue to build my library of people, events, and experiences. I would have to include Vince among my rarest books, although I never knew his last name.

I didn't spend too many weeks in the bowling alley before my dad caught up with me. He kept his temper in check, but his face was livid when he walked me to school, his strong hand firmly placed against my back, propelling me into my class. Again I was in a foreign land without a passport.

At Jefferson Junior High, I discovered what I thought was an innovative way to improve my academics. Girls. I'm not sure what their attraction was to me, but it was obvious that girls were more willing than boys to help me with school subjects.

I thought that if I learned to dance I would earn points with the opposite sex, so I went to the community center on Friday nights not just to jitterbug, but to search for smart-looking 13- and 14-year-old girls. *If they are pretty*, I hoped, *they will also be smart.*

I made the basketball team in seventh grade, but the triumph was short-lived. I was kicked off the team because of my grades. When he heard, my dad stalked into the principal's office with an agenda of accusations.

"You are not being fair," he insisted. "Johnny is a good basketball player. Give him a chance to show what he can do."

But his intervention didn't do any good. It was the school-guard situation all over again. It didn't make any difference how I might excel in other ways. If I couldn't read, I was nobody.

Mr. Nobody began to cut classes more and more. I went back to the bowling alley where I set pins for ten cents a line. I felt protected there, as I did at home. If anyone started to pick on me, Vince would shout, "Deja le solo." He was my friend, my tough guardian angel.

I couldn't explain my hurts to my parents. In fact, I'm not sure I could have put my feelings into words to explain myself to *myself.* I loved my parents and didn't want them to worry about me. My dad was a teacher who consumed words like a hungry man at a huge meal. How could I tell him about the nausea I felt on Friday mornings before a spelling test? He was always running to football or baseball practice, rushing home to feed the family, running off at night to a second job. My mother had the household duties for a large family and left for work in the afternoon. We were not unlike many families today, racing to stretch the paycheck.

In seventh and eighth grades, I didn't really know what I was doing right or wrong. I challenged authority, but it wasn't the unbridled defiance we see today, with kids carrying guns to school. Rather, it was the type of rebellion that made school hostile territory and the bowling alley safe. Without a family who loved me — though not understanding the source of my turmoil — I might have turned out like many kids in our inner cities for whom gangs are substitutes for real families.

I always seemed to find a way to make money. I loved to work. When I saw the fruits of my efforts it was a good feeling. Since we lived near a university, I went to the football games and hawked peanuts and Cokes. I could buy a Coke for six cents and sell it for ten, so the games were profitable. However, the football games opened my eyes to a new threat from authority figures. The college kids knew how to spike a Coke, so by halftime many of them were pretty high. In fact, tips were much higher in the second half. I'll never forget one game when two older boys, about 19 or 20, walked up to me and grabbed me by the neck as the bigger one said, "Apologize to my girlfriend for what you said."

"I don't know what you're talking about," I shouted, looking around for the source of his jealous rage.

They pulled me into the tunnel behind the stands and began to accuse me of insulting his girl.

"Let go of me," I yelled. "Who are you?"

My tormentor showed me an ID card with a picture on it. "Look, kid, I'm a cop. Here's my card." I couldn't read what it said, so I just gaped at him. But I didn't believe he was a policeman.

The adult literate world is the enemy. They have power over me.

He began to pull my hair and demanded an answer or apology. I was on my knees, with my head beginning to scream from pain, but I wouldn't answer. Just then, a uniformed campus policeman walked by.

"Hey, get this beast off me. Help!" I howled. He glanced at us briefly but just kept walking. My anger against authority figures was compounded.

Two college girls, evidently the guys' dates, came out of the stands and pleaded, "Don't hurt the kid, he didn't do anything—let him go." They watched for a few minutes and then left, leaving me to deal with the overbearing jerk who had had too much to drink.

His buddy kept saying, "Let go of the punk—we'll miss the rest of the game."

The game ended and my abuser released me with a few ugly epithets. I felt as if I had won a battle against injustice, even though my scalp raged. As I ran away, my last words to this college punk were "I hope you enjoyed the game, you coward."

When I told my son this story years later, he said, "Why didn't you just apologize, Dad?" I guess it was because I knew intuitively that he wasn't going to hurt me. He had searched me for a weapon and had asked if I had a knife. I figured he was as afraid of me as I was of him. The guy was big and strong, but I had as much will to control him as he had to control me.

My son didn't understand this encounter any more than I did at the time. I was fed up with the adult community, and this bully represented their ugly side.

How easily a young person can be jettisoned into a pattern of anger when he feels his self-worth is destroyed. I was a volcano, calm as Mount Saint Helens before it erupted, but sending out seismic warnings far in advance.

My parents thought my pattern of truancy and failing grades could be broken if I returned to a Catholic school, so they enrolled me in St. Mary's, one of the largest parochial schools in Albuquerque. One day the nun announced to the class that we were going to have our pictures taken on Wednesday. "Be sure to wear the proper attire," she said, "or don't expect to have your picture in the yearbook." Proper attire meant no T-shirts. They were considered underwear and entirely inappropriate. So I skipped school that Wednesday.

The next day I got it. The teacher called on me and said, "You were absent yesterday. Where's your note from home?"

I didn't stand up, nor did I answer. Two inexcusable acts of disobedience. All eyes were upon me — nobody ever defied the nuns so audaciously.

"Stand up when I'm speaking," she said with a voice that sounded like she had her teeth clenched. "Why did you play hooky?"

"You said if I didn't have a shirt with a collar, I wouldn't have my picture taken. I don't have one."

Her eyes took in my well-bleached T-shirt and the pants that barely skimmed my ankles, and I knew I had pushed the right button. Now she would feel sorry for me. Sure enough, it wasn't long before the nuns sent home some shirts and a suit for me. But I was embarrassed because I had humiliated my parents with a charity handout.

I had found the power to confront, and for the first time I thought I could pull the strings that would make the literate world dance. Play the fool, cultivate the right friends, defy or beat the bullies, challenge the adults. The pattern of my life was beginning to unfold.

I was moved to another class, which is often an acceptable way for teachers to get rid of troublemakers. There I met Sister Ruth Agnes, my homeroom, math, and English teacher — my nemesis. This five-foot, 100-pound woman who always wore black but never a smile also was in charge of the Altar Boys Society. At noon she was the "head warden" of the cafeteria. I'm sure she wished she had never met me.

Any hopes of fulfilling my dreams of becoming an altar boy — a prestigious honor — were squelched in the third week of school by Sister Ruth Agnes. She made and enforced the Society's rules, and the academic standards were high — too high for a kid like me.

Boys who can't read need not apply.

In the cafeteria Sister Ruth Agnes and I were in total agreement. I didn't need the warden to tell me that children in Europe were starving and it was a sin to waste food. My appetite made it easy for me to obey that rule. She would patrol up and down the rows and search the lunch trays for signs of leftover food. I tried to sit next to my little sister Michele, a finicky eater who lived in fear of being forced to eat everything on her plate. To my delight, she would pass her unwanted vegetables under the table. We might have been breaking the rules, but somehow we thought we were helping the starving children in Europe.

I was failing in English, but in math I was the second-best student in the class. This was as black and white an issue as the nun's habit. My answers were correct 90 percent of the time, and I knew I deserved a B+ on my report card. I could add, subtract, and do multiplication tables, though I couldn't grasp word problems. Anthony was my friend, I thought, so I let him copy my math homework. On report card day, I eagerly anticipated my good grade in math. When I opened it, I saw all Ds and Fs. *Where is my B in math?* Anthony got a B with all the same answers — *my* answers.

When the bell rang, I remained seated while all of my classmates quietly filed out of the room. Sister Ruth Agnes closed the door, turned around, and saw me at my desk — the kid who was usually the first to run outside.

"Johnny Corcoran," she said in a tone that said "Come up to my desk."

I walked to the front of the room, and said, "Sister, you made a mistake on my report card."

"I don't think so," she replied, without looking at my card. "If you're referring to that math grade, you have a bad attitude. Besides, your sister wasn't good in math either. That will be all."

That hanging judge wasn't going to consider the facts — appeal denied. "Close the door behind you," she mumbled. (It sounded more like a growl.)

As I walked out of the room feeling cheated, I had to decide whether to leave the door open or slam it as hard as I could. I closed the door quietly.

With that battle ending in defeat, I walked across the playground toward the bus stop, ripping my report card into a thousand little pieces. I put them in my mouth and chewed them to a pulp, holding back my tears of anger and hurt. I spit my pulverized card on the ground, grinding it with my shoe. War was declared.

I hate report card day.

I prayed as I got on the bus, *Please, Jesus, get on this bus with me today. Sit next to me and don't let anyone sit on your lap. I want a seat all to ourselves.*

The city buses were always noisy, especially at this time of the day when the public schools got out and the university students had late afternoon classes. I plunked my token in the meter and plopped down in the one open seat, right behind the bus driver. I hated that seat, but at least all the kids from school were in the back. I didn't have to listen to them say, "What did you get on your report card?" "I'll let you see my card if you let me see yours." My favorite seat was the seat next to the rear-door exit, where I could watch each person as he got off and where, at the end of the line, I could be out in two seconds flat.

My moves were predictable and my pattern was to seat-hop until my seat was open. My changing seats seemed to irritate the old grizzly who drove the bus, but that wasn't my intention. I just liked to sit in my special place. Why did he care where I sat?

It's a public bus and a free world, isn't it? I hate report card days.

I had to get report cards off my mind, so I thought about the time I trapped the old bear. That was a great day. I was enjoying my favorite seat — it only took three moves to get there — when I noticed the unsmiling driver was looking through his rearview mirror at me. I wasn't making any noise, but I figured he must have just come out of hibernation and wanted to eat a kid for dinner.

Who knows? I wished he would keep his eyes on the road instead of looking at me.

I'll give him something to look at.

I slowly took my pencil out of my pocket with my right hand, giving the bear enough time to see that it was a pencil, opened the window, and with weapon in hand, put my forearm outside and pretended to write on the side of the bus. I deserved to be nominated for an Oscar, my performance was so convincing. At the next stop, the driver got off the bus carrying a two-foot steel bar he used to check the tires. He walked around the bus, checking the front tires first and then walking to the left rear. I watched the drama unfolding as if I had written the script myself. I leaned out the window to see him checking the right rear tire, or was he looking for the evidence? Surprise! Clean as a whistle.

"Do we have a flat tire?" I asked. He looked up at me without expression, but I think I heard a groan like a wounded bear. What a great day!

But it is still report card day. I hate report card day!

ONE TIME WHEN I was absent from school, Sister Ruth Agnes told the class, "Don't laugh at John — there's something wrong with him." Of course, one of the kids told me and I thought, *Someday she's going to pay.*

Less than a week later, a new boy joined our class. His name was Vinnie, a transfer student from Pittsburgh, a likable guy with a distinctive Eastern accent. One day when Vinnie was out of school with a cold, Sister Ruth Agnes took the opportunity to share with the class that Vinnie was a convert to Christianity and was studying his new faith. She said, "Now, boys and girls, I want you all to be good role models and make a special effort to make him feel at home."

I couldn't believe this was the same person who told the class that something was wrong with me. She wanted to make the new kid feel good, but it was okay to make me feel lousy. She ended her remarks by telling us not to mention this to Vinnie.

When Vinnie returned to class, my buddies and I invited him to eat lunch with us. We were all brown-bagging it that day, so we found a place under a tree on the school grounds to eat and "make Vinnie feel welcome."

I appointed myself head of the "welcoming committee" by saying, "Sister told us that you are from Pittsburgh, Pennsylvania, and that you were a convict."

"That's a lie! I've never even been in trouble. Why would Sister say such a thing?"

"Your secret is safe with us; we won't hold your record against you. Please don't say anything to Sister. She made us promise not to tell you."

We weren't in class more than five minutes before Vinnie raised his hand and asked, "Did you tell the class I was a convict?"

Sister Ruth Agnes looked shocked. "Oh, no, I said you were a *convert*." She looked at me with fire in her eyes, and I stared right back with an innocent expression that wasn't very convincing. Oh boy, was it satisfying for the second-best math student in the class to embarrass the enemy. She never again talked about students when they were absent. But she frequently had my desk moved out in the hallway, which suited me fine. I was like a pebble in the bottom of her shoe, and she needed to get rid of me in order to maintain control in the classroom.

THE YEAR WAS 1953, when bobby socks and baby boomers were the order of the day, and our educational system was considered the best in the world. Or was it? It was two years before Rudolf Flesch wrote his revealing study, *Why Johnny Can't Read*. He could have dedicated his book to me, for I was a kid headed for failure but boiling over with unleashed ambition.

In ninth grade, rival groups fought against each other at school. They weren't organized into gangs like young thugs today, but they fought hard for their turf and their honor, whatever that was. One lunch period, Anthony told me that Romero, the meanest, toughest kid in town, was after me. His clique had the reputation of beating up any kid he didn't like. I tried to keep out of sight, but when it was time to return to class, there was no escape. Imagine my shock when Anthony, my buddy, came up and punched me in the jaw. I knew he must have defected to the other side and the enemy would be close behind. Sure enough, with fists up and blood in his eyes, Romero came from his lair behind the cathedral. I ducked the first blow and he missed. I was saved by the school bell, and the nuns (whom I irreverently called the Penguin Gestapo) came out to round us up for class. Romero, who was completely intimidated by Sister Ruth

Agnes, moved into line. But instead of complying with protocol, I headed straight for Anthony, my personal Benedict Arnold, and gave him the beating of his life right in front of the nuns. It wasn't a wise thing to do.

Now they knew for sure that something was wrong with me. I was violent and dangerous. Sister Ruth Agnes was so outraged by my behavior that she sent me to the principal, Sister Mary Catherine, who told me that I would stay after school and wash all the windows in the convent. (She was a friend of my dad's, so I got off easy.)

If Sister Mary Catherine hadn't interceded, I probably would have been expelled. She was a sign of God's divine mercy toward me, an immigrant from the Emerald Isle, with blue eyes that sparkled and a smile to match. She greeted all the kids each morning as they filed on the school grounds as if they were her own flesh and blood.

"Top of the mornin' to you, young Mr. Corcoran. Looks like a good day for the Irish. And can we expect the best from a fine lad from the Corcoran clan today?"

"Oh, yes, Sister," I would say. She could disarm me in a minute.

She was almost six feet tall and was someone I had to look up to. My "Irish connection" was the head nun, the boss lady. Even Sister Ruth Agnes called her Mother Superior, which gave me a sense of security.

The afternoon of my punishment, one of the older nuns, Sister Naomi, watched how I worked hard on the windows, and asked, "Would you do me a favor?"

"Of course, Sister," I said. She was one of the nuns I respected.

She asked me to put the curtains up in her room after I finished my penance, and I made certain they were hung straight and neat. She was pleased with my extra efforts and persuaded Sister Ruth Agnes to give me another chance.

I was transferred into Sister Naomi's English class, and I vowed to be a model student. I managed to give oral book reports by asking one of the avid readers, usually a girl who spent her extra time in the library, about a book she had read. I'd remember the name of the book, stand up with cards in my hand, and proceed to tell the title, the author, the setting, and the story. Somehow, in my warped logic, I didn't think this was cheating. I just thought I was defying a system that wouldn't or couldn't teach me.

When there was written homework, I would copy from someone's workbook or have a girl write it for me, and when it came to tests, I didn't cheat. I simply didn't take them.

For Sister Naomi's sake, I tried to behave; however, one day I said something insolent, and her unpremeditated reaction was to slap me. I was so angry with myself for being disrespectful to someone who had been so kind to me, and so hurt that she would strike me, that I automatically returned to my dumb kid theatrics and fell to the floor, intentionally pulling my desk on top of me, playing like a wounded cowboy who had toppled from his horse. The class giggled, and once more I thought I had controlled an encounter. But inside I felt sick with shame. I knew I had destroyed the trust of someone who had believed in me.

CHRISTMAS VACATION WAS a reprieve from the torture chamber. Those precious two weeks were the only present I expected. At the beginning of the vacation, Mother called Patricia, Judy, and me into the kitchen and closed the door. Our two little sisters were playing with paper dolls in the living room.

We knew what was coming because we had heard this lecture before. Mother wiped her hands on her apron and gave a little sigh.

That was a bad sign. "Maureen has been sick a lot this year; the doctor and medicine bills have been very high."

Oh-oh, here it comes.

"We just don't have the money to buy any gifts," she continued, "except a little something for Michele and Maureen because they're young and don't understand." She made a stab at being positive. "You three can choose between having a Christmas tree or a turkey."

"What will we have if we don't have turkey?" I asked. Food was one of my favorite subjects.

"Probably meat loaf."

Meat loaf for Christmas dinner? No leftovers? "My vote is for turkey," I announced decisively.

"Me, too — we can always make Christmas decorations," Patricia said.

We both looked at Judy. It seemed like ages before she answered. "Turkey...I vote for turkey," she proclaimed as if her vote was a tie breaker.

"Of course, you'll get your gifts from Aunt Dorothy. And my friend Jane said she was going to drop by this afternoon with a little something for you," Mother said with new cheerfulness.

We searched in the hall closet for the few Christmas decorations we had and found a roll of paper with a brick pattern imprinted on it. "I got an idea," Patricia said, "let's make a chimney."

"Yeah, so Santa Claus can come down it." We snickered at my ridiculous joke, knowing that Santa Claus was broke this year.

We were working on our chimney when Jane arrived, and Mother took her into the kitchen for a cup of coffee.

"She didn't have any presents with her," I whispered to my sisters. Patricia gave me a "shut-up" look.

"Children, come into the kitchen," Mother called.

Jane pulled out some envelopes from her purse and said, "I have something for you kids."

"What is it?" Michele asked.

"Well, it's a picture," Jane answered, giving each one of us a plain white envelope. Judy opened hers first and pulled out a crisp new one dollar bill. The rest of us looked in our envelopes and we all had one. A dollar was a fortune to us, and to have one of our very own was a big treat.

"A picture?" I said.

"Of course, a picture of George Washington, our first president."

A couple of days later, Patricia said to Judy and me, "Let's buy a present for Mama and Daddy with the money Jane gave us." After discussing several impossible ideas, like a new easy chair, an electric mixer, or even a TV, my little sister Michele said, "They need money."

We decided to pool all our "pictures," put them in a big box, and wrap it up as a surprise. This was going to be a great Christmas!

Three days before Christmas, my dad and I went to our local gas station. When we pulled up to the pump, the attendant said, "Hey, we've had the drawing for the TV; haven't you been collecting tickets?" We sure had. For every dollar of gas we bought in the past few months we had received one ticket. We must have had at least 25 tickets at home. We wrote down the number of the winning ticket and took it home to compare with ours.

I pulled our tickets out of the kitchen drawer and looked at all the numbers. 10834. *What am I seeing? 10834!*

"Dad, Dad — Mama — Patricia — Judy — wow! We won! We won! — We won!"

My dad came into the room, took a look at the number we had written down, and announced, "Get in the car — we're going for a ride!"

We went back to the gas station, laughing and shouting all the way. We put the TV in the back of our '47 Plymouth station wagon and I sat holding it next to me, with my legs hanging over the open tailgate and my sisters crowded around me. We yelled to the passengers in other cars and pedestrians on the sidewalks, "We won! We won a TV! Merry Christmas!"

On Christmas morning we were in church and I whispered to Patricia, "I bet we're the only people on La Luz Street who have a TV."

"No, the Petersons have one. Now be quiet."

Yeah, but they bought theirs. Ours came from heaven in time for Jesus' birthday. Merry Christmas, God.

Of the 2.4 million who graduate from high school each year, 25 percent cannot read or write at the eighth-grade or 'functionally literate' level. The estimated cost of U.S. students repeating a grade in school because of poor reading skills is two billion dollars annually.

— Business Week, special report September 18, 1988

CHAPTER 6

The Great Deception

WHEN I LEFT ST. MARY'S at the end of ninth grade, I was a confused kid, believing in God, but not believing He could help me read. Sure, He gave us a TV, but that wasn't like the gift of words. Maybe if I could read some of the instructions He had in His book, I might be able to find out what He wanted me to do. *If I could read.*

Imagine what it would be like to climb on a magic carpet and land in China without an interpreter to try to read the street signs or a menu in a restaurant. That was the way I saw the English language. Lines without meaning. Isolated words out of context.

Today millions of English-speaking American kids enter high school unable to interpret the simplest directions, graduating without knowing how to fill out an elementary job application. They stumble through true and false tests, copy from the kid across the aisle, or play a guessing game that might give them a passing mark.

Sometimes they use signals, one finger for true, two for false. Multiple-choice questions have a code: The number of fingers indicates whether the answer is A, B, C, or D. I knew those tricks. I used all of them and even more.

I couldn't distinguish between drain cleaner and scouring powder, except by the pictures on the label. How could I know if I was getting aspirin or a sleeping tablet? Is that restroom for men or women? *(Was the shorter word* men?*)*

When I entered high school, there weren't any studies or national surveys about illiteracy. But I knew how I felt about myself, and it wasn't positive. Dumb, ignored or dismissed by teachers, evasive, polarized by literate and illiterate camps, angry, and confused.

In Catholic high school, I was a troublemaker. I continued to live a double standard: dutiful son and fun-loving brother at home; wary, defensive adolescent at school. I seemed to attract fights.

I remember Denny, a belligerent kid who whipped me twice in my freshman year in a knock-down confrontation. Red-eyed revenge was in my blood. On Friday night there was a dance at school, and Denny came into the lobby of the gym with his entourage. Hands in pockets, sarcastic smiles on their faces, they swaggered in like they owned the place.

"Make way, Blue Eyes," he said as his buddies laughed at me. They had seen my downfall at the hands of their leader.

Tossing aside all good judgment, I headed for Denny like a pit bull chasing a cat and slugged him three times before he knew what had happened. Father Stephen, principal of the school, was standing a few feet from us. It was like speeding past a highway patrol car in a red Corvette.

"Johnny Corcoran," Father Stephen said as he grabbed me by the collar of my blue suede jacket, "you are to leave the dance immediately."

Denny glared at me as I skulked out the building; the wide eyes of his gang followed my humiliating retreat.

Just before the dance was over, I sneaked back into the gym, looking for my taunter. With his supporters scattered, Denny knew I was out for blood, so he ducked out the side door and later spread the word around school that I was crazy. *Loco.* Where had I heard that before?

LAYER BY LAYER, my self-esteem was stripped away like the leaves of an artichoke. I desperately needed recognition, as every kid does, so once again I used my athletic ability in an attempt to prove I was good at something. I went out for basketball, but because of my insubordinate attitude toward the coach, I was not only kicked off the team but expelled from school.

"Johnny, why do you get into fights?" my father asked. "I know you're a good kid, so what's wrong with you in school?" The hurt in his eyes was intense, but I couldn't explain my emotions.

"I don't know. I really don't like to fight," I answered, staring at my size 12 shoes. He would never understand the seething hostility within me. I couldn't tell him I had reached high school and still couldn't read. I wanted to cry like a baby, but I didn't know why I fought like a tiger.

When my father walked me into the office of Highland High, I knew he was humiliated over my behavior; nevertheless, he stood by me. If he had given up on me, I might have dropped out of school at that stage. I didn't want to continue embarrassing him, so I made another vow to listen to my teachers, to respect authority, and to keep my fists to myself.

Mr. Kinsey was a gift from God in the new school. He was another major book in my library. I felt that he really liked me. He gave me the encouragement I needed, even recommending me for a job as janitor in charge of a highway patrol office. I got up at 4:00 A.M. and made a whopping dollar an hour. In all of my experience, it was the first time a male teacher had shown confidence and belief in me. Out of all the kids he could have recommended, he chose me.

At Highland I had a friend, Charlie, who worked with me on a system to pass every test. Our cheating skills were slick, but my conscience was eating at me. One day I told Mr. Kinsey I had cheated on a test and didn't deserve a B. He simply said, "Well, don't do it again." He never reprimanded either Charlie or me, and he continued to trust us.

But I couldn't stop cheating. I was like an addict, caught in a compulsive behavior that I hated but ignorant of where to find a cure.

When Mr. Kinsey lectured in the sociology class and evaluated us on our oral participation, I earned good grades. But I began to cut the classes that required reading and writing, and eventually I was sent to the counseling office to be tested.

Now what do they want to know? Am I a psychopath?

The oral questions were a cinch, and arranging blocks in design patterns was elementary. I think they were looking for some way to document that I was mentally retarded so I could fit into a nice little category. When I passed the test, I felt I had upset their apple carts.

My report cards began to look better, because my cheating ability was becoming a science. I could not decode words, but I took advantage of my talents, trusted my intuitive thinking, and invented solutions to problems. I used my audiovisual senses to learn. Radio, movies, television, and pictures in *National Geographic, Look,* and *Life* became my substitute textbooks. I developed good listening habits, and when the better students were daydreaming, I paid very close attention, just as a deaf person does to a signer.

Toward the end of that 10th-grade year, my dad acquired a job in Ajo, a small copper-mining town in the Arizona desert. Packing up, saying good-byes, and moving on like migrant workers in the fields of education were common experiences; but this time I welcomed the change. It was time to leave Albuquerque and break the cycle of fighting and failure.

Where can I find the key to unlock the possibilities in my mind?

How long would I be like an artist with a roomful of paints but no paintbrushes; or like a secretary with a word processor without a keyboard? Something that was so commonplace to others was lost on me. If no one could help me fill the gaps in my ability to comprehend letters and words, I decided to invent my own methods of coping.

I was like the gunfighter in the old Western movies who would say, "I wanna hang up m'gun and start over."

As determined as I was to have a clean slate in my new school, I soon was caught by Mrs. Roberts, the English and literature teacher, in a compromising situation. She had high expectations of every student, and that included me.

It was Monday morning and she was returning our essays titled *Sir Winston Churchill.* I had turned in my assignment (which had been written by Mary, another student) on Friday. The graded papers were handed back, except for mine. Mrs. Roberts said to me, "John Corcoran, come with me. We're going to the principal's office."

She gave the class a stern warning about misbehaving in her absence and led me out of the room, down the hall to my public hanging. She marched me right into his office and began to carry on at length about the derogatory statements I had written about the great statesman.

At least she thinks I wrote it. But what did I say?

I got an F on the essay and had to spend an hour in the principal's office. To this day I don't know what Mary wrote about Sir Winston Churchill. But it obviously wasn't good.

AJO WAS A new book in my developing library. "Reading" it gave me an insight into some of the experiences of life in a small town and a small high school. I was determined to turn my life around and become an insider. Most of my school years I had felt like an outsider, but I had become a keen observer of the kids who were the in-group and I began to act the part. I associated with the popular clique and the academic achievers, played three sports, and was in the Letterman's Club. I became campaign manager for a student who was running for student body president. I even participated in the school Christmas play as one of the wise men. What a joke! I loved it.

Our time in Ajo was a brief, cleansing shower after a dirty trip. It was a record year for me with only two fights and perfect attendance. Once I had decided that I couldn't beat the system, I learned to invent my own learning strategy. Why should I be a Buzzard when I had the ability to be an eagle?

Ajo in Spanish means garlic, which has a pungent odor and taste as well as certain healing properties. That's a good description of the effect Ajo had on me.

Every move in my adolescent life seemed to bring a new character out of me. I thought if I played the strong, silent type, I would keep them guessing. I might even be considered a deep thinker. But one incident in Ajo burns in my memory like a physical blow to an abused child. I was sitting in study hall with Alfred, a new friend, intently "reading" a magazine, when he suddenly grabbed it out of my hand and jokingly announced with a loud voice, "What do you want that for? You can't read, anyway!"

I jumped up from chair, snatched the magazine out of his hand and said, "If you want to keep your front teeth, don't ever do that when I'm reading."

I don't think he knew I couldn't read; but what he intended as a kidding remark hit a nerve. Somehow I felt betrayed. He was no longer a friend, but a quisling.

DURING MY JUNIOR year in high school something happened that increased the load of responsibility in our family. Overnight the eight Corcorans became 11.

Late one night we got the kind of phone call that jerks you out of a sound sleep and makes you sit up in bed with your heart pounding. I heard my mother say, "Who is it, Jack?"

"It's Marilyn." About ten minutes passed before he said, "She needs help. I'm going to Roswell. Don't worry."

My older sister, Marilyn, was married with three little girls and lived several hundred miles away. Father didn't give me any explanation. He just walked into my room and said, "Get up, Johnny. I need you and Patricia to help me drive to Roswell. We'll be back in three days. Take what you need."

That's a 16-hour drive! Our car won't make it.

I dragged myself out of bed while Mother packed some sandwiches and fruit for the three of us. As we went out the door, I looked at the clock. It was midnight.

I was 16 and silently questioned the sanity of my father. *He has a college degree, but I don't think he's very smart. Help, I need another family! These people are nuts!*

"John, are you awake enough to drive?"

"Yeah, sure."

Patricia took the keys from Dad and said, "Here, I'll drive."

Patricia always has to drive first.

I stretched out in the backseat of our 1950 Buick, thinking, *What a joke. We'll never make it on these tires.*

"Patricia, let me use your pillow while you're driving."

"Okay, but when Dad's driving, I get it."

Sisters. What a pain.

I fell asleep and woke up to bumping sounds. We were driving on the side of the road, off the blacktop. I knew it — we had a flat tire. The moon was so bright when we piled out of the car that we didn't need our flashlight. Good thing. The batteries were dead.

Dad and I had the spare tire on in Indy 500 time. I got behind the wheel and asked a logical question: "Do you think we can make it to Roswell and back with these tires and no spare?"

"We'll make it," Dad said, with the same confidence he gave his football teams. Ten minutes later our headlights went out. I pulled off the road and opened the hood, but we knew this was something we couldn't fix. "It'll be light in an hour, let's get some rest."

Is this what the luck of the Irish is all about?

When the sun came up, I started the car and began to drive while my father and sister dozed. A short time later Dad looked at the speedometer and said, "Keep it under 50. That donut we just put on the front didn't look too good." My dad always called tires donuts, and about that time a real one would have tasted great. As this wonderful idea came into my head, the "donut" blew out. "No spare," I mumbled as I pulled off the blacktop.

"Dad, what are we going to do?" Patricia sounded like she was going to cry.

"Well, it's only flat on the bottom," I said. No one laughed. *I didn't even think I was funny.*

Ever optimistic, Dad said, "Get in the car. It's only about ten miles to the next town. We'll make it."

I had seen people driving on a rim before and I always thought they were stupid, crazy, or poor. I was sure we were all three.

When we chugged into the next town and found a gas station, Father said, "Fill 'er up and look under the hood."

The attendant stared at us and asked, "What about the flat tire, Mister?"

Dad looked down as if he had just discovered something new and said, "Oh, my son and I will take care of it."

I couldn't believe him. *Doesn't he remember we blew out the spare, too?* If this was meant to have been an adventure, I wished he had chosen a better route.

After negotiating the price of a used tire down from five dollars to two for seven dollars we went on our way, trusting in the "magic man" who always seemed to pull us out of tight spots. As we drove on, he finally broke the silence about this trip and said, "Marilyn and the kids are waiting for us and we need to get there as soon as possible."

After a few minutes, my sister said, "Daddy, you know this isn't the first time he's hit Marilyn."

"I know... but I hope it will be the last."

I was shocked. I didn't know my brother-in-law had ever hit my sister. Even though I'd been in a lot of fights, I didn't understand a man hitting a woman.

We made it to Roswell, and my sister was packed and ready to leave. I played with my three nieces while Father went for a ride in our car with my soon-to-be ex-brother-in-law. I never knew what was discussed, but when we left there were four brand new tires on the old Buick.

On the return trip I was driving again and glanced in the rearview mirror to see my sister and her three children asleep, snuggled together peacefully. I thought, *We may be poor, but we're not stupid or crazy.*

WE MOVED TO Parker, Arizona, before my senior year in high school. That's when I met Mildred. I was hauling hay for a farmer, and she ushered at the one movie theater in town. I spent a lot of money that summer on movies and sodas at the local drugstore. Neither one of us smoked, drank, or attended any of the notorious local parties, so our parents approved of our dating. Before the summer was over, Mildred was wearing my class ring and we were going steady.

When the fall term started, she was head majorette for the marching band, and I was on the football team. One important obstacle loomed in our young romance, however. She was one of the smartest girls in the school, enrolled in the college prep courses. That five-foot-six brunette with blue eyes was also prom princess, salad bowl princess, and student body secretary. She was the best shorthand and typing student in the school. (The yearbook predicted she would become a secretary at the United Nations headquarters and win national acclaim because of her accurate note taking.)

I knew that God could perform miracles, so I began to pray that one day I would wake up, grab a book, and begin to read. All of the letters would make sense, the sentences would flow together in a wonderful story, and I might even be able to read poetry to Mildred.

I made friends quickly at my new high school. After all, I was Mildred's boyfriend and had the size and physique for football. For once, I was *somebody*.

Athletes were the insiders at school. I was on the varsity team, which was the top of the social heap. One class, however, was particularly intimidating. Bookkeeping. Fortunately, Mildred was in the class too, and since I was good at math, she would read the questions and I worked out the figures. I looked at her with the lovesick eyes of a high school boy, and said in my ah-shucks Gary Cooper voice, "Mildred, read me that problem; I'll show you how to solve it." After all, she was my girl, so she would oblige my request. I don't think she ever guessed my secret.

I had been elected homecoming king during the football season. It was actually a popularity contest, and the votes that pushed me over the top were from the Indian and Mexican kids, two groups I knew well and liked. My two best buddies were Merle, an Indian, and Tino, a Mexican. After football season, I made the basketball team and was in my glory.

Just as our basketball team was close to the championship and I was the leading scorer, my dad took a job in Blythe, California, 60 miles away. He had worked on his California teaching credentials by going to night school. He knew the opportunities and pay were higher in California, plus, he and Mother hoped the climate would be better for my sister Maureen's asthma.

He taught me that education is a lifelong commitment: "Remember, Johnny, it's never too late to learn."

I was in the middle of my senior year. *How could I leave Mildred? What about the basketball team?* "You can stay in Parker and I'll commute," my father said. Ingrained in our family, however, was the idea that families stick together, so I chose to go with them.

In spite of that decision, I was filled with resentment. I was tired of having my life disrupted and was sick of moving. I *wanted* that championship, and I didn't want to leave my valedictorian girlfriend.

I kissed Mildred good-bye and left the team short a high-scoring player and leading rebounder. I hated the idea of moving to Blythe, but I placed family loyalty first. I didn't know that I was headed for another heartsickening blow from the school authorities.

THE MOVE TO California was the beginning of a westward dream that my parents had shared for years. I realize now how God orchestrated that journey, even though it was a bitter pill for me at the time. Marilyn was able to find work in Blythe and it was there she met Charles — a fine, hard-working family man who loved her girls and eventually adopted them. Later, they had three more children. Father's job was a step up and, with luck, I would be able to finish high school.

Blythe did offer me one fine experience: the chance to make friends with African Americans, who made up 30 percent of the school population. I knew Indians, Mexicans, and Spanish people, but my new black friends became rich encyclopedias in my expanding library of people, places, and experiences.

If God hadn't endowed me with athletic ability, a gritty sense of survival, and a sense of humor, I don't know how I could have endured finishing high school away from my girlfriend.

As the last days of my senior year approached, I called Mildred with the great news. "Please come to my graduation. There's going to be a big party afterwards and I want to show you off." That would make up for the months of separation.

"Of course I'll come," she said. I was so excited I could have made a free throw with my eyes shut.

I couldn't believe I would actually be receiving my diploma. With my skill in getting people to read and write for me, plus the intense desire to achieve in spite of my handicap, a diploma was assurance that I could succeed.

On commencement day the entire Corcoran family and Mildred were in the audience. I put on horn-rimmed glasses with no lenses, slicked back my hair with baby oil, and marched down the aisle, towering over most of my classmates. The glasses were strictly for show; they made me look more intelligent. That was one day I didn't want to be inconspicuous.

Mother, Father, all my sisters, and Mildred smiled and waved at me as I stood on the stage, waiting for my name to be called. When the principal said "John Corcoran," I stepped forward to accept that precious roll of parchment. I couldn't wait to unroll and frame it.

After the recessional, midst the jubilance of the graduates and their families, I unrolled my diploma to see those magic words, even though I couldn't read them. My eyes began to sting behind the fake glasses. The diploma was blank.

I was in total shock. No one had called to tell me that I needed extra credits or that I was deficient in some subject. They had allowed me to parade across the stage, had my name listed as a graduate, and then sabotaged my reward. I felt the old anger beginning to well up inside.

"What do you make of this?" I asked, passing the empty scroll to my father.

He read out loud the attached note: "'Diploma held for requirements.' Did you know anything about extra requirements, Johnny?"

"No, sir." It was hard to talk.

This was a thousand times more humiliating than the dumb row. Mildred had come to celebrate with me, but I felt like a kid who thought he was getting a bicycle for Christmas and received a bottle of castor oil instead. If Boogie's doghouse had still been available, I would have crawled in.

Father was steaming when he saw my dilemma. He was a teacher in that school — the principal was his boss. Why wasn't he told that his son needed additional credits? We both felt the authorities had hit below the belt.

The standards were not very high; if you behaved yourself you could make Cs or Ds and pass. Low expectations of the staff resulted in low accomplishments among the students. I managed to slide through without the basic skills needed to accomplish anything significant. During the summer I took the class to get the additional credits needed and of course I had to cheat, but before I turned them in, the high school had recounted my credits and sent me my diploma. The irony is that I didn't deserve the diploma in the first place but was denied it because somebody couldn't count. Somehow, I knew that I needed to prove my worth to the establishment.

What could I do? The logical direction for illiterate Johnny at the age of 18 would have been to try out for an athletic team, work with his muscles in some laborer's job, join the service, or become a drifter.

Instead, I decided to go to college.

When a student arrives at the university he finds a bewildering variety of departments and a bewildering variety of courses. And there is no official guidance, no university-wide agreement, about what he should study.

— Allan Bloom, *The Closing of the American Mind*

CHAPTER 7

Fear the College Years

ONE LITTLE VOICE WITHIN ME said, *John, you bluffed your way through high school, but college is big time. You'll never fool those guys.*

Another voice, gritty and determined, answered, *You can't give up now. Prove you have a mind. Go for it!*

My parents never considered that I wouldn't go to college. Mother would pepper her conversation with, "When you go to college...." My dad had degrees or college credits from six different institutions of higher learning and read books like a kid eats popcorn — whole handfuls at a time. He taught school intermittently for 40 years to support his family. He insisted that we speak the King's English, which meant no slang or swearing. Of course his son would go to college. Education was important to him, as was natural curiosity, athletics, and hard work.

I thought, *I can't let my family down.*

In my imagination there were two fields with a fence between them. To get to the literate side where the grass was greener, I needed a passport stamped with the seal of a college diploma that wasn't blank.

Recent studies have shown that even mildly reading-disabled children from supportive homes are prone to be more anxious and less happy than their peers. Also, research indicates that social competence is lower for reading-impaired boys.

I can't say that I was an unhappy person, but certainly I lived on the edge of anxiety. Would my mask be yanked off? Would I be humiliated and degraded before my family and peers? Every day I walked that tightrope, believing there was no net to keep me from certain destruction.

When the white literate society talks about illiteracy, it usually refers to the economically and culturally disadvantaged, or to ethnic and racial minorities. Although I did experience economic poverty in my childhood, Mother and Father were loving, supportive parents, and their commitment to us was a priority in their lives. I couldn't disappoint them.

Years later, after my father had a stroke and couldn't talk, I would go to his house and tell him what I was doing. He would cheer me on without words. When my business was on the skids, he communicated in his silent manner, "We trust you." That's what he had done even when I was coming home from school with bad reports; and that trust was the ingredient that ultimately motivated me to continue my education. In my own distorted logic, however, I didn't trust my parents enough to reveal my embarrassing inability to read.

By the time I entered college, I was well into my masquerade. All I had to do was remember what people thought of illiterates. There didn't seem to be any safe harbor for us. We were the dumb ones, the no-goods.

Who could I trust to give me more than just superficial dignity? The schools had their chance to teach me to read when I was in the elementary grades. For the first six years of my schooling, no one uncovered my need. Nothing had changed, except I was more adept at learning and gaining my own education without the basic skills.

I went to two junior colleges in California and plowed through like an explorer wading through mud up to his knees. Mildred went to both schools (I don't know if she followed me or I followed her), and without her I'm not sure I would have made it. She was in many of my classes and did everything she could to help me with my studies. She typed papers I dictated, summarized books for my reports, and encouraged me. She was my survival kit. They say love is blind, and I believe it, because with all the help Mildred gave me, she never knew I couldn't read.

ONE DAY AN amazing offer came. I was presented with a full athletic scholarship — including board, room, and ten dollars cash a month for laundry — to Texas Western College (now the University of Texas in El Paso). A dillar, a dollar. I wasn't even a ten o'clock scholar! But I was six-foot-four, could dunk a basketball, and could at least read the scoreboard.

Facing such an enticing offer, I couldn't turn it down.

When I left Blythe, a small farming town, for the big city of El Paso, I began a sojourn that lasted three years, the longest I had ever stayed at one school. From the way my parents fussed over me, you would have thought I was back at St. Michael's. "Where's your bus ticket? Do you have the train ticket from Phoenix? Do you have the claim tickets for your two trunks? Here's some sandwiches I made."

"It's okay. I'll call you when I get there," I promised. I hugged them both and climbed on the bus, but my thoughts were with Mildred. She wanted to get married, but as smart as she was, I didn't think that was a very smart idea. I wasn't ready.

I desperately wanted a formal education, to be a legitimate insider, but I didn't know how to do it if I couldn't read. I didn't know then that my college years would provide me with a body of lifelong personal knowledge that expanded my library to include some of my most precious and priceless books.

When I first stepped off the train in El Paso, it was the repeat of a familiar feeling: I was the new kid on the block. By this time I had attended 16 different schools.

Maybe I'm over my head this time. I'm a good poker player, but regular college kids get dealt five cards, while a kid who can't read only has three. Good thing I'm a good bluffer.

As I collected my two footlockers, the clerk observed, "Those things weigh a ton."

"How far to Texas Western College from here?" I asked.

"Couple of miles up the hill," he said.

A voice from behind me said, "Hey, do you need a ride?"

A friendly college-age kid gave me a ride to the campus and left me with a "Welcome to TWC." I had arrived.

I struggled up the stairs to my dorm with those two-ton trunks and opened the door to room 210 where I was greeted by a big, friendly guy, "Hi, I'm Jim Morris, your new roomie. The coach asked me to show you the ropes."

My schedule was laid out: Tuesday was a team meeting and orientation for new players; Wednesday I would get my classes.

"Don't worry about not getting the classes you want. Athletes get to preregister. After you get your schedule, we'll pick up your books," he grinned with the confidence of a senior who knew all the ropes. "But this afternoon we'll do the important things — go over to the girls' dorm and check out the new freshmen."

I laughed and wondered how we could tell who the smart ones were.

Dating at TWC would expand my education. Over the next three years I dated more than a dozen very intelligent girls. Kathryn, a Catholic, Glenda, a Southern Baptist, and Gayle, a Jewish coed, provided me with special friendships and an informal class in comparative religions.

New students are usually perplexed about the college environment and challenges, but I was a fish swimming in murky water. I listened to the questions at the registration tables and then picked my subjects. I didn't trust the counselors, so I hung around the athletes and listened to their comments.

"I hear that prof is really tough. Gives surprise quizzes and doesn't grade on the curve. Friend of mine had him last year."

Cross that course off my list. I'd walk along the tables, trying to catch any clues about which class to take and which to avoid.

"He's a soft touch. Lectures all the time. No term papers."

Remarks like those helped me make choices. It was just a matter of staying alert. I signed up for 21 credits and attended classes for three weeks. At the end of that time, we could drop courses without a penalty. I observed the teachers and evaluated their styles; if they gave essay questions or if students read aloud in class, they were probably on my drop list. I pared my credits down to 15 or 16 units and began the next phase of my educational plan. Essays, book reports, and term papers were easy to acquire.

BEING A JOCK had its advantages. I was rushed by the fraternities and joined Sigma Alpha Epsilon, the top academic house on campus. My life was filled with illogical decisions for an illiterate. Fraternity life in the late 1950s taught us social skills and offered a camaraderie I needed. I was glad for Mother's rules because I was ahead of some of my brothers in etiquette and good manners. I was even elected house manager for three terms.

During those fraternity years prejudicial tugs-of-war were played in many Greek houses. I remember one day when three of my fraternity brothers and I were discussing a freshman who was going through rush.

Don, a good buddy from Ohio, said, "Guys, you know Tommy Garcia is going through rush, and I know he would like to pledge SAE. He'd make a great brother."

"With a name like Garcia, he'd be blackballed," Bill said.

"By whom?" I said.

"James for sure, and probably Peter and Edwin."

"No *probably* about it; I've talked to them. They don't even like Mexican food."

My muscles began to tense. This was an old story with a new location, and I didn't like it.

Someone came up with a plan. We would call for a special meeting and not tell the three dissenters about it. The four of us took the active list and each of us recruited four more so we would have a quorum. When our mission was accomplished we asked the president for a special meeting on Sunday night, since that was when one of the dissenters worked.

On Sunday night the meeting was held at 7:00 P.M. The discussion was about Tommy Garcia, and several actives spoke in favor of his being accepted. Everything was going like clockwork when the door swung open and in walked James, Peter, and Edwin.

Bill whispered to me, "How did those jerks find out?"

The president asked if anyone wanted to speak against accepting Tommy. No one spoke.

It was time for the vote. Each member had a white ball and a black ball in his hand. A box was passed around as we dropped a ball into it; three black balls and membership would be denied. When the count was done, there were three black balls in the box.

Don turned to me and said, "Okay, Corcoran, you get the honor of telling Garcia."

I thought of fifth grade in Carlos Gilbert school. *Well, Dolores and Maria, we gave it the old college try.*

FROM THE DAY I registered, I began to plan my strategy. My scholastic criminal career was about to begin. I'm not proud of any of my covert actions, and it has taken me many years to be able to publicly confess them. If there is no honor among thieves, there is certainly no honor among cheaters.

An illiterate person who gives the appearance of reading is always in danger of being discovered. As I began my college years, I realized I would need every ounce of cunning I could muster. I found I could get through a few courses — speech, office machines, typing, and PE — with a minimal amount of cheating. I got a legitimate A in practice teaching math at Austin High School.

Frank Laubach, the visionary leader of the volunteer literacy movement bearing his name, has said, "A literate person is not only an illiterate person who has learned to read and write; he is another person." I wanted to be another person, someone who could understand the names on classroom doors. Was this room for English poetry or basic economics? Was I carrying a sociology, psychology, political science, or philosophy text? No one can understand the struggle within the soul of an illiterate unless he attempts to lead a life without being sure of words on a bottle, a menu, a street sign, a newspaper, a bill, a legal document, or a letter. It's like being blind in a strange room without the benefit of touch.

Mildred became a dim chapter in my book of romance as I began to date one of the smartest girls in school, a beauty queen who was chosen as Miss El Paso. She wore my fraternity pin but never suspected it was an intentional ploy when I asked her to decide what she wanted at the local eatery. When she ordered something on the menu I could easily say, "I'll take the same." I became very adept at dodging and ducking the printed word. Most of the time it was as natural as breathing.

I would do anything to pass my courses. If I could get test answers, I would go to any extreme to copy them before class. It was during that era, I believe, that the term cat burglar became a cultural idiom. I must have seen the movie *To Catch a Thief* starring Cary Grant and Grace Kelly because, with a flair for drama and youthful agility, one night I climbed the fire escape at the faculty office building and crept along a three-inch wide ledge, arms outstretched, my fingers gripping the protruding decorative trim on the side of the building. When I finally reached the window, I pried it open with a butter knife and entered my business administration professor's office. Once inside, it was easy to get copies of the quizzes. With the answers in my pocket, I inched my way back across the ledge and climbed down to the ground.

On one occasion there was a file cabinet that I couldn't open, but I was sure it held a treasure of tests and answers. One of my buddies, who was almost as adept at subterfuge as I was, helped me enter the faculty offices at 3 A.M., carry the cabinet down two flights of stairs and into an off-campus apartment. We called for a locksmith, who swallowed my story of needing to enter the file to get some valuable papers, and he opened it with his special tools. When he left, my buddy and I carried it across campus and back up to the third floor without being caught. That was an act of a desperate young man, and except for the grace of God, I could have been arrested for breaking and entering.

One required course challenged my plans. It was U.S. Government, and the teacher did not have prepared tests I could pilfer. He would write three essay questions on the board and give us two hours to answer. I found my solution in Clarence, a genius-level student with a major crush on my sister Judy. Clarence and I worked out a mutually beneficial exchange of favors. He desperately wanted to take Judy to the SAE formal, and I desperately needed answers to the U.S. Government final.

When the day for finals arrived, I got to class early and found a seat next to the window in the first-floor classroom. I took two blue books to class, one to copy the questions and drop out the window to Clarence, the other to pretend I was writing answers. It took me a long time to laboriously copy the essay questions from the board into one blue book, but when I finished, I slipped it out the window, where Clarence was waiting to catch it. He sat under a tree and easily wrote the essays. Meanwhile, I spent the remaining two hours scribbling in my dummy book. Clarence got a blind date with Judy and I passed my final. Fair exchange.

AT NIGHT I owned the university, since I possessed the master key to all the offices. I was an illiterate outlaw, though it was the type of behavior I hated. I had been brought up to speak and to seek the truth, to be respectful, and to confess my sins. To numb my conscience, I became adept at rationalizing and justifying my actions. In the Bible it says, "For it is written," but not for me.

One night I was caught, an event that could have ended my college career. I was in a professor's office, looking for some test answers, when I heard the custodian speaking Spanish to someone down the hall. I could hear him walk toward the office, so I pressed my six-foot-four, 210-pound body against the door, thinking if he tried to open it, he would think the lock was jammed.

"Abre la puerte — ¿Quien esta alli?" ("Open the door — who's there?")

He pushed, and I held. He was strong, but I had more leverage and staying power. We continued this battle of the bodies, until he finally walked away. His footsteps clicked down the hall and I heard a door close. I waited for what seemed like hours and then walked out. He had tricked me. He was waiting outside.

"What are you doing in there?"

"The door was open and I was looking for Dr. Hart."

He knew I was out of bounds. The thought flashed through my head, *Should I hit him and run?* It was ironic: It wasn't the president of the university or the dean; it was a *custodian* who had the power to wash me out and end my college career only one semester away from graduation.

"How about 20 dollars (which I didn't have) to make you forget you ever saw me?"

"No — no — no!" He shook his head decisively. He was too honorable to accept a bribe.

"Let me explain," I begged. He nodded, locked the door, and then took me to the boiler room where he stored his tools. For a half hour I appealed to his emotions with all the histrionics I could muster.

Knowing the familial closeness of Mexican families, I told him about my large family, my Catholic background, and the extreme embarrassment it would cause them if I were expelled.

Finally he said, "You give me the key — I'll throw it away. Promise you'll never try to break into these offices again."

I handed over the key, thanked him, and promised that I would not steal into an office again.

He never turned me in.

IN MY SENIOR year, the college basketball team voted me their captain. My good friend Don was voted assistant to the captain and was called cocaptain. To be recognized by my peers for leadership was a great honor, and for 24 hours I was elated beyond belief.

Don was the coach's choice for captain, and he was also the favorite with the former coach, then the dean of men. He was liked by faculty because he was a good student and was studying for the ministry. By contrast, I was just a part of the athletic establishment on a scholarship.

The evening after the team vote, my picture was in the newspaper, along with Don's. I couldn't read the story, so was momentarily elated until a teammate said, "Hey...we elected you captain. Looks like the coach did a number on you. The paper says you and Don are *cocaptains*."

I thought maybe he was playing a trick on me, so I just shrugged my shoulders and went to my room. My roommate, who was captain of the football team and a pre-law student, gave me a congratulatory slap on the back and said, "Hey, you were elected cocaptain! Great goin', buddy."

The facts had been confirmed, and I was stunned and confused.

I had confronted many teachers before, but I was too shaken to confront the coach. I sank into depression, somehow blaming myself. It could have happened to anyone, but as an illiterate, I felt powerless to deal with the situation. Maybe the rules had changed, and I didn't get it.

No, I get it—the "authority" had betrayed me again. Athletics was the one world where I believed I could expect fair play. But the newspaper article confirmed that the printed word had wedged its way into my safety zone.

The pain of that rejection took me back to the dumb row. To me, the literate world had once again tugged at my inferiority complex and stabbed me in the back.

Adult illiterates have a common thread in their lives, and it is woven with fear, humiliation, and emotional trauma. I thought I was alone. Certainly everyone in college could read. What was I doing there, anyway?

Nevertheless, basketball was a positive experience, especially the privilege of rooming with Charlie Brown. George McCarthy, the head basketball coach who recruited me, had recruited Charlie, the first black student athlete to play major college basketball in the South and Southwest, two years earlier. He led the Miners to a Border Conference championship in his senior year, which was my first year at El Paso.

Perhaps because we were both from California, the coach assigned me to room with Charlie when we were on the road. He was one of the best players in the country, and I was honored.

On one road trip, we played in the deep South. Normally, we all went out to eat together after the game. We had just won a tight contest, and Charlie had scored the winning point with a free throw.

Back at the hotel, we were gathering in the lobby to go out to eat and unwind a little. Don said, "Where's Charlie?"

"He was still up in our room when I came down," I said.

Another player said, "Hey, do you think he heard those guys calling him nigger?"

"I'm sure he heard it, but he didn't let it get to his game," Don answered.

"I'll go up and get him," I said. When I walked into our room, Charlie was lying on his bed with his hands behind his head, staring at the ceiling.

"Aren't you coming with us?" I asked.

"Nope," he said. "Why don't you bring me back a hamburger and a Coke?"

"Come on, Charlie, everybody's waiting for you. We can't celebrate without you."

"John, just bring me a burger, okay?" He was very serious.

I went out with the rest of the guys, and Don told me about the year before when they played Hardin-Simmons and Charlie was refused a room at the hotel where the team was staying. Because of him, they were told they couldn't eat in the main dining room, so a banquet hall was closed off for them and they were asked to come in the back door.

I returned to the our room early and gave Charlie his food. We talked and laughed for about an hour and finally turned in.

It was quiet for about ten minutes when Charlie said, "Thanks again for the burger and Coke."

"You're welcome, Roomie," I said.

" 'Night, Roomie." The tension had gone out of his voice.

I lay there thinking, *Charlie, I know it's not the same, but I know something about feeling like an outsider — about feeling different.*

Seven years later, in 1965, with five African American players as starters, Texas Western upset basketball powerhouse University of Kentucky to win the National College Athletic Association (NCAA) championship. Charlie Brown, the gentleman, had paved the way for that great victory.

MY FEELINGS ABOUT those years at Texas Western College were ambivalent. I loved the school, but I felt like an intruder, someone who had entered a foreign country without a passport and would be apprehended by the gendarmes at any moment. To this day, I quote one of my favorite professors who said, "If you receive a degree from this institution, along with it goes your obligation to never stop learning."

I am not advocating cheating, because in spite of my degree, I never beat the system. I don't blame people for being suspicious, but the truth is that the system never taught me or caught me.

Many years later, I was speaking at a university in the South and a very irate professor approached me with that you-are-a-fake look in his eyes.

"*Mr.* Corcoran," he said through pursed lips, "there is no way you could have been in a class of mine without being able to read. I cannot believe such a fabrication." (I guess that was another way of calling me a liar.)

"Sir," I replied, knowing that it was difficult for a literate person to grasp the limits another person might go to hide his handicap, "I would not have been in a class of yours. I'm sure I would have dropped out after the first day. You are too astute as a teacher."

Since the good professor still didn't believe me, he wrote the university president. This is a portion of his letter:

Mr. Corcoran spoke at a benefit our local adult literacy pro-
gram sponsored. He claimed he was a very low level of a func-
tional illiterate when he graduated and that he had been
admitted on athletic scholarships. He claimed to have earned
three letters. At least one was in basketball. He also said he
never wrote or read anything in order to graduate and that he
had thought about turning in his teaching 'certificate' to you
since he may have obtained it under false pretenses. He claimed
to have talked about this to you.

We would appreciate your verifying this or denying this.

The president of the University of Texas, Dr. Diana Natalicio, answered my critic by verifying the record. I had, indeed, graduated from Texas Western College in 1961 with a degree in education. Dr. Natalicio called my achievement "an extraordinary scholastic masquerade," and she added, "We at the university welcome his emergence from that closet of illiteracy and support his national efforts to promote adult remedial programs for those who share his previous burden of illiteracy without the exceptional talent to achieve in spite of it."

That letter from the president of my alma mater was very special to me. It did not eradicate my guilt for the tactics I used, but it validated her intellectual integrity as a person who had achieved the highest position in a major educational institution. She did not know, however, about my covert activities.

My response to my critic took me 40 hours of painstaking writing, with the help of a dictionary and thesaurus. At that time, it had been only two years since I had learned to read and write, and I was still struggling with basic language skills.

But I answered the doubting professor: "When I was a young undergraduate student at Texas Western, I was a terribly desperate young man who wanted to be successful in life and in our society. Basic education is mandatory for success and I did not want to be second class or left out.

"My false pretenses, my sins, my crimes, and my trespasses, real or imagined, against literate society are confessed, and I take full responsibility for them and ask the literate society to forgive me."

When my college experience is questioned, I can only reply with the facts, some of which are shameful.

WHEN GRADUATION DAY finally came, my mother and father drove their new car out from California to celebrate the first of their children to graduate from college.

But now what? I faced the same sickening abyss of uncertainty that was there when I graduated from high school. Military service? Professional athlete? Construction worker? All are respectable occupations, all requiring at least some reading ability. No. Instead, I made another illogical choice in my illogical life.

I'll be a teacher.

The secret of teaching is to appear to have known
all your life what you learned this afternoon.

— Author unknown

CHAPTER 8

Master of Masks

M Y COLLEGE DIPLOMA WAS so new it hadn't yet been framed
when I received my first job offer. The El Paso school district
offered me a position for $3,500 a year, which was the starting salary
for a first-year teacher in 1961.

What a joke. If they only knew the real John.

I often felt like I had the last laugh on the literate society, but it
was laced with the pain of my own inadequacy. It was a part of my
defense mechanism.

My parents had moved from Blythe to Encinitas, California,
which was a difficult decision for my dad since he had to take a
$1,600 pay cut and lose his tenure. My dad, the perennial optimist,
said, "This is surely the promised land." The small coastal town in
San Diego County was the final destination of the Corcoran family's
westward movement. The years from 1943 to 1958, times of frugal
living and frequent moves, were only a memory.

They bought a home by the beach, and for the next 30 years provided their children and grandchildren a place for family gatherings,

barbecues, and surf fishing. It was like all the Christmases we had ever missed.

When my dad called from Encinitas and told me of a better job near where they lived, I was excited. He obtained an application and filled out the papers while I dictated the answers over the phone from Texas. He still had no suspicion of my secret.

The salary was a hefty $5,500, plus an extra $300 for coaching two sports, so I headed for California to begin a 17-year teaching and coaching career. This is the point where most people stumble on my story. (But how? That's impossible! There's no way.)

My two worlds were inside and outside. Most people, like Walter Mitty, dream of doing great things with their lives. As a college graduate, I wanted to soar. But my feet were mired in the quicksand of words. I was afraid I would get sucked into oblivion at any moment.

Why did I choose teaching as a profession? Perhaps subconsciously I wanted to prevent children from enduring what I had to endure. I believed in the highest ideals of the teaching profession, best expressed by Anne Sullivan and her student Helen Keller. I believed that teaching was one of the most honorable jobs a person could have, and somewhere in the back of my mind, I thought the school environment would provide me the opportunity to learn to read. I also thought it was a place where I could find respect. It provided job security, summers and holidays off, health benefits, a nice working environment, and incentives to continue my education. The reason I got a degree in education was a coincidence: By the middle of my junior year, the majority of classes I completed I could apply toward a degree in education. Practice teaching was just acting, according to my interpretation, and I had been playing different roles for years.

Einstein, a dyslexic, said that education can get in the way of learning. I approached my teaching job as a learner, but on the first day I was overwhelmed with conflict — not in what I was to teach, but in the absurdity of it all. It was like providing a medic with Band-Aids and sending him onto a battlefield where people were having their legs blown off. I couldn't even read to pronounce the students' names. *Dear God, how am I going to do this?*

The Corcoran seating chart was a survival technique. Before school started, the teachers would receive a master list of everyone who was coming into their classes. When the students arrived on the first day, I had a blank seating chart prepared, with squares on the chart for each desk. After they took their seats (sometimes there was a scramble because many had special friends they wanted to sit next to), I would go to each desk and say, "Are you in the right class? This is room 101, first-period sophomore social studies."

"Yes, sir."

"What is your name?"

"Anne Sanders."

"Anne, please print your name clearly right here in the box where your seat is on the chart." I would stand over her shoulder to make sure she wrote in the correct box. Then I picked up her pack of cards indicating her schedule, initial my class card, and pass to the next desk, until all 30 students were checked off. This procedure would take most of the first day of class.

I could then compare their names with the names on the master list I had received from the office, and tell who was absent. This was a painstaking task, comparing each name, letter by letter, line by line. The whole process was terrifying and time consuming at first.

On the second day of school, instead of calling role as most teachers did and having the students answer, "Present," I would say, "Class, I want each of you to call out your name, loud and clear, so all of us can get to know each other."

Within a week, I could learn 30 or more names without reading a list. Later I improved my system by having a student aide check the roll and write down those who were absent for the day.

Each day presented another challenge to cope with my illiteracy. Carlsbad High consisted of four plain stucco, single-story classrooms, a two-year-old facility in a coastal community that took great pride in its first high school. Classes were small and the staff was close. New teachers were conspicuous. I immediately applied my professional look and wore a suit and tie to work every day, kept my brand-new 1961 Mercury Comet polished, and walked with a no-nonsense stride. I was 23, outwardly confident, pleasant, cooperative, and I liked kids. But I was cotton-mouthed scared.

THE PRINCIPAL ARBITRARILY assigned me my classes: sophomore social studies and English grammar. The first day I arrived early and stayed late, a habit I maintained for the duration of my teaching career. I hoped I would learn to read, but first I merely wanted to survive and not attract negative attention, especially during the first few years. Later on, I would became more bold.

To create the illusion of literacy, I always tucked a newspaper under my arm or carried books as props. In the faculty room, I listened to teachers' complaints and grievances; discussions and debates were sometimes stimulating, sometimes inspiring, and other times depressing. I would pick up information about current events by listening to other teachers talk about the front-page news. Not believing everything I read in the newspaper was not my problem; rather, it was trying to evaluate their biases and prejudices, sorting out not only what they said, but also their political persuasions. I was trying to learn my lines and act out the part, not unlike an aspiring young actor observing and listening to the master actors on a movie set.

When I stood before my first class, my selfish motivation for embracing this profession began to melt. I couldn't teach those kids to read, which made me as guilty as the teachers I criticized. However, I could teach them to be learners, to have positive experiences in their lives, to believe in their own unique abilities. My prayers were frequent and repetitive: *God, help me to teach these young people . . . and bring someone to help me. God, please help me learn to read.*

As a student, I had been a keen observer in the classroom, remembering what made good or bad relationships between students and teachers. I had done everything in this drama — the props, the sound, and the lights — but now I was on center stage. I had a degree that said I knew what I was doing. At least I thought that's what it said.

The fact is, most education courses required for a teaching credential do little to provide classroom teachers with the proficiency or knowledge to teach reading or writing skills. Many new teachers, literate or illiterate, either sink or swim on their own. If it hadn't been for Susan Struggs, surely a gift from God, I probably would have quit teaching in the first 60 days.

Susan was one of the brightest students I ever had, and she literally propelled me through sophomore English. I'd shuffle the papers on my desk, and then say, "Susan, will you please read from the spelling workbook today?" She became my right hand. I put her in charge of the tests and assigned her the list of words to be used; she even graded the papers. She was my teaching partner, and since she was so much brighter and more mature than her classmates, this arrangement was acceptable to them.

When we studied literature, Susan would read a chapter a week from a famous American author. I discovered some of the magic of Mark Twain, John Steinbeck, and others; we laughed over *Huckleberry Finn* and followed the migrants in *Grapes of Wrath*. A few other kids started to volunteer to take turns reading, but I was keenly aware of individuals, like myself, who were petrified at the prospect. I was determined not to cheat these kids out of a positive learning experience, but I was haunted by the fact that if they couldn't read and write, they would have difficulties competing in school or in the workplace.

If I could write a book, I'd have some stories to tell! But then, I can't read, so how can I write?

I usually evaluated students orally. I developed my listening skills and interviewed each of my students formally and informally.

One year, I required each of my students to meet with me during lunch, or before or after school, for 15 to 30 minutes. I learned a lot about young people and was surprised when most of them said, "I've never sat down and just talked with a teacher."

"It wasn't so bad, was it?" I would ask.

Most of the time they would say, "It was great, Mr. Corcoran. Thanks."

When I did give written work, the students graded one another. I received questioning looks from some who wondered why I didn't do this work myself, but they knew I was a recent college graduate and liked me because I treated them differently from the way other teachers treated them.

Without consciously knowing it, I was creating a student-centered learning environment that developed out of my own desperation and need. I placed the educational responsibility on the students, teaching them to become peer teachers to one another. That was a break from the ordinary pattern in those days, and it created new ways of gaining knowledge that conformed to the way I had learned.

In the fable of *The Emperor's New Clothes*, one small child revealed that the king was naked. I lived each day wondering who would say, "Mr. Corcoran can't read." But no one did. Every day a bulletin was handed to the teachers during second period. Instructions were "Teachers only read the bulletin. Do not let the students read this." I would hand it to one of my brighter students and ask them to read the announcements. Then the giggles would start. "Mr. Corcoran, it says we're not supposed to read the bulletin."

I had to tell kids to break the rules. "Never mind, just read it." Fortunately, neither the principal nor other teachers came in during that time.

Sometimes my students thought I was kidding when I would mispronounce a word. It was the game of "Let's catch Corcoran because he's good for a joke."

"Okay, class, today we're going to take a trip to the libary [sic]."

Gary, a good-natured, quick-witted college prep student, would give me a funny grin that usually indicated I had cracked a joke.

"Hey, Mr. Corcoran, when are we going to the libary [sic] again?" he would tease, with a laugh that could be heard the length of a hall. For six months he kidded me for mispronouncing that word, but he never realized the discovery he had made. I felt like I wasn't getting the punch line, but I couldn't ask him what it was. The joke was on me and I knew it.

By the second semester I heard the subtle difference in the pronunciation. Lib–*r*–ary. This experience happened many times. I learned proper pronunciation and new words from Gary and other students who were my unsuspecting teachers.

It wasn't until many years later that I found out that hearing sounds and relating them to letters was the ten-ton stumbling block in my reading perception.

At the end of my first year at Carlsbad High, I decided that I was going to quit teaching. The pressure was too great. I cautiously went into the principal's office to turn in my resignation.

"Mr. Robinson, I don't feel qualified to teach English. I love the kids, but I'm not being fair to them."

He was an intelligent man who had majored in English. He had once told me that he liked what he saw of my work but suspected that I had a literacy problem. My heart pounded with fear, until I realized that he suspected everyone. Most of the teachers were terrified of him and his exacting standards; he was always correcting the teachers' communication. (Today, I believe that up to 25 percent of all teachers may have some degree of language processing problems that could be diagnosed and treated.)

The principal sat behind his desk for what seemed an eternity before he finally looked up at me. *He's guessed that I can't read. Now my goose is cooked.* "Corcoran," he said, "you came to Carlsbad High and turned a losing basketball team into a winner. Also, the kids like and respect you. Tell you what: Instead of English, why don't you teach world history next fall? You're going to make a good teacher."

Saved by the bell! World history would be a snap. There are probably more films on world history in educational film libraries than any other subject, and I knew more about history than I did the English language.

"Thank you, Mr. Robinson," I said. I had thought he could see right through me. Living a lie is like carrying a boulder on your back; any moment you can stumble and fall.

But I stayed on at Carlsbad, and my students and I saw *many* educational films that year.

A TEACHER USUALLY is buried in paperwork, but I handled all the reports, grades, and letters by having students do them. At first I was critical of myself for using them this way, but I rationalized that they were learning to do real projects in the real world. In one class, I dictated letters that the students took down in shorthand or longhand and then typed. I always had any correspondence to the principal proofread by a student or by my father.

When I went to Carlsbad, I had aspirations of being the head varsity coach. But I realized that the man who held the job had no intention of leaving, so I began to look around for a more satisfying position. I feigned a sprained wrist (complete with bandages that I had applied myself), and asked a friend to fill out a teaching application for me, which I copied and sent to numerous schools around California. The one that intrigued me the most was a town called Corcoran. I was attracted to the name, but was particularly drawn to the salary: $7,500 a year, plus an extra $600 for coaching. My prayers were answered when I got the reply from the school. I handed the letter to my dad, knowing he would be amused by the coincidence of names.

"John, this is great! You got a varsity coaching job!"

Until he congratulated me, I didn't know whether I had been rejected or accepted. Dad never realized the extent of my illiteracy. Surely he must have thought it strange that my speech was peppered with unfinished sentences and mispronounced words.

Perhaps he and my mother loved me so much that they chose to overlook those idiosyncracies. Maybe they were in denial. I just don't know.

Corcoran, California, was a small farming community with an old two-story high school building. I was hired to teach bookkeeping, social studies, and physical education. Another plus was my position as head varsity basketball coach. The town had a large population of

Mexican laborers who worked in the fertile fields of the San Joaquin Valley. The school contained some of the same elements as Carlos Gilbert in Santa Fe. Here, too, anger boiled in young people and self-esteem dragged on the ground. There were corners where hostile kids gathered in packs.

The turf was familiar. I sold the flashy Corvette I had purchased after my first year of teaching and became one of the crowd. The majority of the 35 kids in my social studies class were illiterate, so my teaching techniques became more inventive as we spent most of our class time in oral dialogue.

My evaluation of a teacher's duties was colored by my own background. A teacher should instill a love of learning in his students. A teacher should stimulate them to discover their individual talents and gifts. Most of all, a teacher should love his students. I had been brought up with the stories of Jesus, and I knew that His disciples didn't always understand what He taught. Those fellows had the greatest teacher the world has ever known, but they weren't the smartest students. But Jesus loved them anyway.

I looked at my obstinate, sassy, sometimes defiant kids and prayed that I could love them with one small degree of Christ's love. But no matter how much I loved them, I couldn't teach them how to read. I was a good motivator, but the cold reality was that I wasn't prepared to do my job. I just couldn't deliver the goods to the customers.

Many of the families in this area were migrant workers who desperately lacked basic language skills. Out of all the students in my social studies class, there were probably only three who could read the textbook. *Oh-oh*, I thought. *I'm in trouble.*

Robert — a disciplined, bright, handsome young man — was the only one who could read well, which made for a prickly situation. To complicate matters, absenteeism was extremely high at the beginning of the school year because, on any given day, half the class were in the fields picking or chopping cotton. I remember one day when Robert asked in frustration, "Doesn't anybody else around here know how to read?" Although he didn't know it, his question included me.

My career as varsity basketball coach began with a thud when the best team in the league beat us by 45 points. We were playing them again after Christmas that year, and I thought we could win if we outfoxed them. Our team was no match for theirs, but I had a plan.

There were two gymnasiums at our school, and while the crowd watched the visiting team, with their six-foot-eight center, go through their pregame warm-up in the new boys' gym, our team was out of sight, warming up in the girls' gym. Normally, both teams warmed up on the same court.

When our team didn't appear for either the 15-minute warm-up or for the introduction of the starters just before the game, everyone wondered where we were.

"What's with the Corcoran team? Are they scared?"

"Where are they? They know they don't have a chance against us!"

"They can't even find their own gym."

But they didn't know that I had a plan.

The officials came looking for us, the crowd began to murmur, and the opposing team was puzzled. When the game buzzer sounded, our kids shuffled to the bench with heads down and expressions sober. The picture of defeat. Our starters walked slowly onto the floor and positioned themselves.

It looked like a hopeless situation. So I took a calculated risk and played a long shot, something I had to do many times in my life.

The whistle blew and our boys were like bullets shot out of a gun. By the time the first half was over, we were ahead by 15 points and their star player had four fouls. The other team thought we were going to be pushovers, but we surprised them — even more, we surprised ourselves. We battled to a win by one point in the final minute. Everyone went wild!

In the stands that night was a perky little Portuguese woman by the name of Kathleen Mendes, who was my blind date after the game. She thought I was arrogant and crazy, and I guess she was right. I was often forced to solve problems in different ways — doing unorthodox things was routine for me, although I often risked being the fool.

Shortly after our big win, the team and I were boarding the bus, ready to leave for a Saturday game out of town. Mario, one of our leading players, hadn't shown up. We were about ready to leave without him when he came strolling toward me with his head down and eyes on the ground.

"Come on, Mario," I shouted, "We've got to go."

"I'm sorry, Mr. Corcoran, but I can't play today. I gotta work in the fields with my dad."

I was dumbfounded. Mario's father didn't understand or respect what his son was trying to accomplish as an athlete. My first impulse was to protest to his father, especially since I knew how much the game meant to Mario. To me, the team came first. But Mario, with the resolve of an obedient son, turned quietly and walked to his father's pickup.

Tyron was another one of my starters who didn't show up for the bus. I was furious. At least he could have talked to me, like Mario. Later I heard that it was because he didn't have athletic shoes — someone had stolen his and he didn't have the money for new ones. When I saw him, I lectured him about his responsibility to me and the team — but I also bought him a pair of shoes, telling him that an interested person had donated them.

Mario and Tyron represented the dilemma I constantly faced.

How could I expect those boys to admit they didn't have shoes or pledge total commitment to the team when I myself didn't come forward with the truth?

I realized that I didn't want to hide my illiteracy for the rest of my life by being a coach. I didn't want to be a dumb jock. I wanted to do something more.

Within me was the plea, *Don't be fooled. The masks I wear are not really me. Pretending is just second nature, but if I give you the impression that I'm secure, unruffled — don't believe me. It's all a sham. If someone would only liberate me from my self-built prison walls. Remove my mask, accept me, love me. But I'm afraid.*

So I played the game of pretend, with a facade of assurance without and a trembling child within. I did not dare let down my barriers.

MY LIFE AND future changed after that blind date. Kathy was a senior at Fresno State, and a weekend romance developed rapidly. I thought she was the cutest, smartest female I had ever met, and she even laughed at my jokes. We would talk and play the game of hearts by the hour, and although I was a very competitive person, it became harder for me to concentrate on the cards.

When we fell in love, I wondered if I dared give her the only key to my secret lockbox. Would this literate girl with the jet-black eyes turn away from me, pity me, or, even worse, laugh at me? I knew she felt the same way about marriage as I did — that it is a lifelong commitment. Honesty had to be part of our relationship. I had always been a risk-taker, but this was the most important risk of my life.

Would she be blown away if she knew I was a teacher who couldn't read?

And now have I become your enemy
because I tell you the truth?
    — Galatians 4:16 (*The Living Bible*)

CHAPTER 9

Speaking the Truth...in Love

"I CAN'T READ. I *CAN'T* READ. *I* can't read." For six weeks I stared at myself in the mirror and repeated those words. I needed to rehearse for the perfect moment to remove my mask in front of Kathy and allow her to see me for the fraud I was. She was a college honor student with a scientific mind, so how could I ask her to marry me without revealing my secret?

When we met on a blind date the night of that one-point-win basketball game, my first impression was *She's too small.* She said she stared at me and thought, *He's too tall.* As the months went by and our relationship became serious, I realized that I had to allow her to see my weaknesses. My reading deficiencies were not obvious; they were hidden, like some rare disease.

I knew that if I opened the floodgates of my inadequacy, I would have to face the consequences of potential disaster. One night after a dinner date, we were sitting in the living room at her grandfather's house, and I knew the time had arrived to say those dreaded words. I put my arm across the back of the couch, trying to be nonchalant.

"Kathy, I have something to tell you."

None of the fights I had been in were as frightening as that moment.

"*I can't read.*" There—I said it.

At first she didn't respond. She had no way of foreseeing the emotional and psychological impact of how my illiteracy would influence every aspect of our life together. I thought that if an educated woman knew she was going to marry a man who couldn't read or write, she would have serious second thoughts. Instead she disclosed her own heartache. She looked up at me and said, "I'm Rh negative."

Both of us sat there crying, revealing our innermost fears. I didn't understand the Rh negative factor, and she thought my confession meant I couldn't read *well*—after all, I had been teaching for three years. Kathy knew I was intelligent long before she understood I was illiterate, so the biased stereotype that illiterates are dumb did not influence her total acceptance of me. I realize now, however, that she had no idea of the extent of my illiteracy; nor did I fully realize how deep her concern was about Rh negative blood type, which sometimes seriously jeopardizes an unborn child.

With a family history of many miscarriages, stillbirths, and preemies that died, Kathy's Rh negative factor felt like a curse to her, and she didn't know if a man would understand her fears. (Years later, when our second baby died, I understood her concerns.)

I had kept my own secret for good reasons. Many people in our society react negatively to handicapped and minority people. If I had told anybody, I probably wouldn't have been able to accomplish the things I did, nor have a beautiful and intelligent woman fall in love with me.

But after our mutual confessions, we had a wonderful courtship and a beautiful wedding, and we were married with the blessing of both families, a great blend of Irish and Portuguese.

Both of us came from traditional Catholic backgrounds and agreed on basic values. Her parents were delighted even more that she was marrying a teacher.

WE SPENT OUR first year in Torrance, California, in an apartment with a swimming pool and a king-size bed. It was a honeymoon where nothing could go wrong. As newlyweds, we saved our money, had no debts, and both worked. Our favorite pastime was paint-by-number. We would snuggle down in bed, shut away from the world, and paint away, happy as children in a sandbox. Obviously, I couldn't work crossword puzzles or play Scrabble.

That year in Torrance presented me with the perfect career opportunity. All I taught was physical education in addition to being junior varsity basketball coach and assistant varsity coach for championship teams. I didn't have the constant pressure of the classroom, and the parent support system was outstanding. I loved the accolades, but inside I was developing a love-hate relationship with athletics. I didn't want to continue as just another jock. If I stayed in the classroom, I thought that might be a catalyst for reading, that somehow words and sentences would suddenly leap into my brain and that everything would be as clear as the dawn after a dark night.

Despite my inadequacies, I felt I had something valuable to offer, which was the ability to stimulate young minds. What I prized the most — reading and writing — I thought were elusive, but almost within my reach. It was like smelling the aroma of bread baking and knowing the bakery must be nearby.

I needed another chance at teaching.

When we left Torrance to move back to Carlsbad (where I would be teaching at Oceanside High), I knew I was taking a calculated risk. But it was something I had to prove to myself. Kathy had her degree in nursing and found a good position with the public health department in Oceanside.

We bought our first little house, and Kathy, the literate member of the family, wanted me to arrange the details of the purchase. It took a high level of trust to close that transaction, but the sellers, parents of a former student of mine, took care of all of the paperwork, including escrow. I negotiated orally and they filled out the forms. This simple arrangement became my training ground and confidence-builder for the years ahead.

When our daughter Colleen was born, she was a healthy, bright child. However, on that evening when Colleen was three years old and Kathy discovered I couldn't even read a child's storybook, I became even more dependent on my wife. She became part of my charade, loving me enough to write my letters, read the documents that were important, and help me maintain my dignity, but still not knowing what was going on inside of me.

Johnny was born, an additional blessing after losing our second baby, and Kathy's Rh fears lessened.

After a time, Kathy filled out applications and I received four National Science Foundation grants. These allowed me to take Kathy and the kids each summer on seven-week working vacations at different college locations. I seemed to excel among my peers at those times, which gave me a deep sense of satisfaction. It's amazing that very little reading was required during any of those sojourns, a fact for which I was extremely grateful.

I was highly motivated to learn, and professors seemed to appreciate having me in their classes. I was not afraid to ask questions, but I often wondered if I would have known the answers had I read the text. In my own classes, I always told my students, "There are no stupid questions. We are all smart and dumb in different ways."

In 1970, before widespread public awareness of child abuse, I was at Louisiana State University when the professor asked if anyone knew why a parent would abuse a child. No one answered. He asked if anyone could guess why. After a short silence, I said, "Because the parents were abused themselves." The whole class laughed, and I was embarrassed — until the professor said, "Mr. Corcoran is correct." I vividly remember that small incident because it was such a great feeling to have the right answer in a class.

During another grad course at LSU, I wasn't so lucky. The teaching style there was more traditional than progressive, and I was sitting next to a nun in class when an essay question was assigned. I looked at her, she smiled at me, but the fear and guilt in my soul overwhelmed me. Of course, I couldn't ask to copy her paper. I was no longer an undergraduate student who could pass his blue book and have it returned with answers; I was a teacher in a graduate class. My stomach began to churn and I said, "Excuse me," jumped out of my seat, and raced for the door. I made it to the men's room just fast enough to lose my lunch there.

One summer Kathy, the children, and I went to the University of Santa Clara on a grant. I spent seven weeks as a student among 40 other secondary-school teachers. The curriculum required interaction with students, conceptual thinking, and game-playing — methods that were natural for me. With all the oral discussions and no required books or papers, I didn't have to fake it. I even earned an A without cheating. As a result, I took a new attitude and energy back to my high school classrooms.

Teaching was my passion, although it was not in the conventional method of readin', 'ritin', and 'rithmetic, the first two of which I knew nothing. What I wanted to do was reach kids and help them discover that they could like themselves and one another. I had a very good rapport with most of my students whether they were categorized as college prep or at risk, but I especially identified with the pain of the nonreaders. I wanted to teach them tenacity and hard work, but their deficiencies in basic skills were overwhelming. I knew what they needed, but I couldn't give it to them.

By the mid-seventies, I was more mature and confident, having observed the system for some time and having discovered that education could go beyond the three Rs. I moved further away from tradition and began to wing it, basing my work entirely on the needs of a class as I perceived it at any given moment. Progressive education was in full swing, and its unorthodox methods suited me.

I began to make my classes more student-centered, pushing the kids into sharing their ideas and dreams. I asked them for their opinions and did my best to build fires under them. Sometimes we soared, and sometimes we crashed; I taught them, and they taught me. We learned and we grew — together.

WE MOVED TO Oceanside, near Camp Pendleton Marine base, where the community and the schools reflected the ethnic and racial mixture of the military. The high school had an interesting multicultural student body: African Americans, Filipinos, Anglos, Samoans, Hispanics, and Vietnamese. As each new class came together, the various groups naturally slipped into comfortable ethnic cliques. Sometimes I would look up from my desk and see a human checkerboard: a square of black, a square of yellow, a square of brown, a square of white, each with an invisible fence around it. This did not always make for an amiable class situation.

No other teacher wanted the ethnic studies class, so I volunteered. This was a district mandated subject, intended to give students insight into the diversity in ethnic backgrounds, problems that arise from differences, and an appreciation of other cultures and their history. "Good fences make good neighbors" was a theory I wanted to dispel.

To break through this cultural isolation, I divided the class into pairs. A Hispanic sat with a Samoan, an African American with an Anglo, a Filipino with a Vietnamese. I would give them 15 minutes to just talk to each other. I encouraged them to share simple information, such as their names, where they lived, how long they had been in Oceanside, and what their parents did for a living. For most of them, this simple exercise was very painful at first.

We didn't solve America's racial problems, but we sincerely worked on them in our own personal way. The year after my first ethnic studies class, I was asked by the Black Student Union to be their faculty advisor.

Later, I took the class on a field trip to the beach (that's a California-style assignment). It was my hope that a change in the environment, away from hostile classrooms, would encourage the students to open up to one another. I asked them to walk in pairs along the sand and talk about anything they wanted. I urged them to share their feelings and investigate what they wanted and expected from class, the school, or the big world outside.

Slowly the class began to meld.

Other days in ethnic studies I might try what I called the *mirror process*. I would say, "Now, I want you to give me your impression of my eyes."

After the embarrassed giggles subsided, someone would say, "I think they're kinda' weird."

When they stopped laughing, someone would get bolder. "I don't feel real comfortable when you look at me."

"Well, I think your eyes are beautiful," one of the girls would answer to the hoots of the boys.

"Now I'll tell you what I think of my eyes. I've always liked them. I've learned you can say a lot of things with your eyes, without saying anything."

After I finished with my opinion, I'd move down to my nose, and say, "I've always thought it was too big." Some of the kids would begin to defend it. To hear someone describe my nose in flattering terms was usually more than I could handle. When we were all laughing, I would pull out Kathy's hand mirror and give it to one of the students.

"Now, I want each one of you to look at your reflection in the mirror and describe what you see. Try to be objective and not make positive or negative remarks. Just describe your face like you would report the details of the face of a bank robber to a police artist." It was almost an impossible task. For many teenagers, their appearance was so connected to their identity that trying to describe their faces was like trying to describe their souls.

At first some of the students couldn't even look into the mirror. But each time we did this exercise, the kids seemed more willing to communicate. They began to feel safe in the classroom environment, even developing a trust in their fellow students. They began to respect one another's privacy, yet to talk to each other about things they didn't usually discuss. For some of them, just talking was a milestone.

Another communication technique was using my children's blocks. I would position the students by pairs, back to back, and give each of them identical sets of blocks of all sizes and colors. One person would then instruct the other how to place the blocks, all the time building his own set. Pedro might say to Carrie, "Take the yellow triangle block and put it on top the long black one. Then place the red square on the right side of the black block," and so on, until I called time. Then they would turn around and compare their piles of blocks. Almost no one placed the blocks exactly as he was told. Why couldn't a person who received instruction follow the directions?

I tried to demonstrate how oral communication could break down even when we were trying our best to make ourselves understood, and how important it was to make it very clear what we were saying.

One student, in his simple wisdom, taught me something about interracial respect. The class discussion was centered around what methods of identification were least offensive. I asked this student, "Wayne, what would you prefer to be called — black or Afro-American?"

"Just Wayne would be okay, Mr. Corcoran. When I'm older, I'd like to be Mr. Johnson or maybe Dr. Johnson."

Wayne was a young man ahead of his time.

Breaking down racial and ethnic barriers was one of the goals in my teaching career. Some of the techniques I attempted were successful; others weren't.

On the basketball court, all my classroom tensions were released. I could be in command without fear of disclosure or reprisal of my illiteracy. There were always, however, other challenges.

For example, it was a tradition for the captain of the basketball team to escort the homecoming queen during halftime of the homecoming game. Michael, an African American, was captain one year and the homecoming queen was white. There was some discussion among the team members about changing the tradition and voting on another escort. The matter was insignificant to me (I just wanted to get on with practice), but the team began to pressure me to let them vote again. In all fairness, I don't believe they were racially motivated. I knew some of those boys would have done almost anything to parade that beautiful girl in front of their friends and families. However, I said, "No way — we're not changing the tradition."

The incident was reminiscent of the time I was chosen captain of the basketball team by my teammates but was demoted by the coach because he thought someone else was a better role model for the athletic establishment. The institution played dirty, and in my invisible illiterate world, I had to deal repeatedly with the pain of what I thought were injustices. I had wanted my teachers or my coaches to stand up for me — but they didn't. I was not going to perpetuate those kind of scars in other young people's lives if I could help it. My students deserved better.

Michael escorted the homecoming queen, and I felt vindicated.

ATHLETIC ACTIVITY WAS beginning to consume me. One day my eight-year-old son came home from Little League practice with a story that gave me more insight into my own growing discontent.

He walked into the house and threw down his mitt. "How did it go?" I asked, noticing his long face.

"The coach hit fly balls to us."

"How did you do?" Sometimes we have to pull the responses from little boys.

"I caught three."

"That's great!" I said. But it was obvious that something else was bothering him.

"But, Dad, Paul dropped one."

"Well, that's why you practice," I interrupted.

"But, Dad...the coach went nuts. He yelled and cussed at Paul. It was scary."

I started to say that coaches yell a lot, when he said, "Dad, you know Paul didn't want to drop the ball. So why did the coach yell at him?"

What could I say? I tried to explain, but we both knew his coach was taking athletics too seriously at that point. I stopped and thought, *Am I making athletics the focal point of my life?*

I loved coaching, but even after producing four winning seasons, including two undefeated championship teams, the seeds of disenchantment were beginning to germinate. My competitive spirit was eroding and sapping my energy. I realized later that it didn't have so much to do with sports (because there are many valuable lessons to be taught and learned from competitive sports), but with an internal conflict raging in my soul. I wanted to be a normal teacher who could read. The lessons I was trying to teach my students in the classrooms made me more and more aware of my own hypocrisy.

I didn't want to hide or get lost inside of athletics, so I began to gradually phase them out of my life. But before I hung up my sneakers for the last time, I volunteered to coach our school's first competitive varsity and junior varsity girls' basketball teams. (No one else had applied for the positions.) It was great to be part of groundbreaking programs that allowed the "other half" to have an opportunity to compete at levels that were previously not available to them. My library was enriched, and many great lessons and memories were recorded in my book titled *More to Learn*.

Colleen and Johnny traveled with the girls' team on the bus and built their own memory books. I taught the girls to play like the boys, saying, "Let's run, gun, and have fun!" We had two sisters on the team who averaged over 50 points a game between them! My five sisters had prepared me to some degree for this experience, but like most men, I still had a lot more to learn about women.

EVERY DAY THAT I taught my classes presented new challenges. Probably half the kids in that high school were intellectual dropouts; their bodies showed up, but their minds were shut down. They were called at-risk students, but I always felt they could be reached.

I was like a blind man feeling his way around a room or a deaf person reading lips. I made up for my inability to read by developing other skills. We would have group discussions, bring in outside speakers, and use standardized tests with an answer key where holes are punched through for the right answers.

In some classes, it was not uncommon for up to 50 percent of my high school students to be unable to read past a third-grade level. I helped them learn the way I had learned. But during all those years I avoided facing the real problem in their lives as well as mine. Still today one of the real shortcomings of progressive education is the de-emphasizing of basic skills.

I don't know what the apostle Paul's thorn in the flesh was, but it didn't seem to keep him from traveling and teaching. He was shipwrecked, beaten, and ridiculed, but he kept going. I am not presuming to liken myself to that great man, but my thorn in the flesh was a daily reminder of how I hurt. Still, I didn't believe in giving up.

In my early teaching years, I primarily taught PE and business classes; in the later years, I generally taught social studies, which included ethnic studies and sociology. I also coached football teams and coached men's and women's basketball in three school districts at five different high schools. Not once in my 17 years did I receive a poor evaluation.

I believe all teachers who are not teaching their pupils to read, write, and spell are cheating them. In that respect, I am certainly guilty. However, if any of my students learned racial tolerance, acquired communication skills, or gained some degree of self-worth,

I believe my teaching was worthwhile. I wanted to instill in those kids the will to succeed, along with a respect for themselves and their fellow man.

Word began to circulate that Mr. Corcoran's classes were fun. To some, fun meant easy. But in a few short weeks it was clear to my students that, yes, classes were often fun — but I also demanded participation. Either they leaped in with both feet and took part or they got out. I had no trouble with discipline.

Many people have asked how I could have been a successful teacher for so long without knowing the basic skills. Stoney and Gloria DeMent have been educators and school administrators in the public school systems for more than 30 years and now conduct workshops on learning disabilities. Gloria evaluated my teaching methods:

John was a master teacher because he did not fit the mold from which I came. For instance, my reading skills were acquired so easily and naturally that I don't recall a single struggle there. Some children acquire reading and language skills as naturally as little birds learn to fly.

I am a visual learner. I must see it to remember it. Being a so-called successful student all through school, I was motivated to stay in that comfortable environment and become a teacher. Most of us teach the way we learn best. My classroom offered too many visual experiences, until I learned more about learning differences.

My husband and John are auditory learners. They must hear it to remember it. They are both excellent in math. My math skills are wretched and my auditory memory is not strong. Clearly, I would not have been the best teacher for those little boys who had very different strengths and weaknesses, who stored, processed, and produced information differently. If teachers do not understand this, they are in trouble and may not be able to see their students reach their potential in their school years, even though they try with all their hearts to achieve this.

When John chose to become a teacher, he knew painfully well what it was like to want to achieve in a quest for learning, only to fail again. He knew what caused suffering for him. He recognized that just as people have different faces, shapes, and coloring, they also have brains which are programmed to function differently. He did not understand his own problem at this point, but he knew that a unique teaching style would be used in his classroom in order to make the most of his own strengths while attempting to meet the academic needs of his diversified students.

John was very aware of his own capabilities and shortcomings, something every teacher and student needs to seriously address. Without special training, he used multisensory teaching techniques that gave his students visual, auditory, and tactile/kinesthetic experiences of seeing, hearing, and feeling. He encouraged exchanges of ideas, interaction, peer partnership. He gave each student the opportunity to enjoy classroom experiences which were successful. This improved self-esteem for all and fostered an ever-deepening interest in class participation. Student teachers were soon sent to John to observe his very effective teaching techniques.

It is true that John's creative approach to school paperwork was unorthodox, but this was a necessary survival skill he was forced to develop. Dyslexics, often being very bright, become very skilled at covering up their lack of language skills. John's story reveals his giftedness, his incredible sensitivity to individual human differences, and his devoted passion for trying to make wrongs come right for himself and others. He never used ridicule on his students. He tried to strengthen their areas of weakness in a nonthreatening way.

The school system failed John and millions like him in a cruel way...mostly out of ignorance. I was honored as an outstanding teacher long ago, but I look back and realize that I failed to meet the needs of some dyslexic children who passed through my life before I was taught how to recognize and work with this type of learner. Sadly, too many adults like John still feel that they failed school.

Why do people want to read? Why does not being able to read eat at so many children and adults in our society, gnawing away at their self-worth like some unseen cancer? Jonathan Kozol, author of the best-seller *Illiterate America*, said the three main reasons people want to read are: first, to read the Bible; second, to read books and newspapers; and third, to help their children. Those were my reasons too, but they seemed so unattainable.

During my young adulthood and teaching years I didn't know anyone in my situation: a middle-class college graduate, teacher, and family man who could neither read nor write. I associated the poor, the underprivileged, and the foreigner with illiteracy. I felt like the only inhabitant on a deserted island in the middle of a hostile sea. In spite of my wonderful wife and children, I was emotionally isolated and depressed.

Everywhere I looked there were words, mocking me, embarrassing me. I would stare at the books on my shelves and wish they would suddenly come alive, speak to me, shout some wonderful truths. But they were as silent as a bank vault behind heavy security doors, silent books for a grown man still sitting in the dumb row.

Kathy never betrayed me. When I talked with someone, I would often dominate the conversation, answering a simple question or remark with a long explanation. I used a lot of analogies to make a point; some were good, some confusing. I know there were many times when she wished I would just say what I meant and not ramble like a broken record. Other times I left out significant phrases or words and didn't make myself understood. At those times Kathy felt she had to explain what I had just attempted to say. I didn't want to be rude; I was just trying to sort out my thoughts. My language processing difficulties not only showed up in the written word, but also in my oral skills. Living daily with those frustrations was like having a continuous itch I couldn't scratch. While illiterates have no outward signs of their problems, they are just as disabled as those with more visible handicaps.

I wanted to break out and live the truth, but my chains were too strong. My constant prayer was for a miracle or a miracle worker because I knew that was the only way I would ever learn to read.

Although there are millions who could use some help, literacy defies counting, because people who are not literate usually hide their pain; they pretend they can read. —Walter Anderson, *Read with Me*

CHAPTER 10

Desperate Behavior

WOULD MY CHILDREN grow up not knowing how to read? My worst fear was that somehow I would pass to Colleen and John a deficiency that would haunt them all their lives. Were there such things as nonreading genes?

Before Colleen and Johnny started kindergarten, I would take them to the library for the story hour. They would come skipping out with a big smile, exclaiming, "Daddy, look at the books I got." I felt as if I had given them a gift, something I didn't have. My children never knew I couldn't read or write.

When our children entered school, we made a decision that Kathy would help them with reading, writing, and spelling, and I would tutor them in math. It was a reasonable arrangement the children accepted without question.

To Kathy, my problems seemed minor, similar to someone with a visible handicap who is able to function so well you never notice his impairment. Since I looked confident and successful, she didn't realize how negatively my self-image was affected. If she had known when we first met how illiterate I was, chances are there would have been little opportunity for me to demonstrate my natural intelligence because she would have begun with the stereotype that says illiterates are dumb.

I didn't trust anyone to totally understand something that was so confusing to me, so I kept my secret. In the 1970s, I never would have asked anyone to teach me to read, primarily because I didn't really believe I could learn, and secondarily because I would have put my livelihood at risk.

After school, I would watch television news for a couple of hours and then pick up the newspaper, trying to match what Walter Cronkite said to words in print. This was futile and frustrating, but I continued to do it every night. I had heard that some people like Abraham Lincoln and Malcolm X taught themselves to read, but it wasn't meant for me.

I kept trying to find reading skills any way I could without giving myself away. Once I started a class in speed-reading at the local junior college, thinking that might work. It seems ludicrous now, but it wasn't laughable then.

Kathy and I went to book fairs and garage sales, adding books to my shelves like collectors' items. I would spend hours turning pages, picking out a word or two, but not enough to put together a complete sentence. I thought if I owned and looked at enough books, reading was going to come to me through osmosis. I bought hundreds of paperbacks related to social studies and ethnic studies for my students to borrow or keep. I loved it when the students read those books at home, and I loved hearing my own children read. But inside I would shout, *Why can't I?*

Colleen was able to read when she was in a Carlsbad Montessori preschool. We were advised to keep her there because at that time area public schools were not teaching reading in kindergarten, except for one school in Oceanside. We owned a small rental house near that school, so Kathy and I decided to remodel and enlarge it to make a nice home for our family. We began the period we called "the house that love built."

This was an American do-it-ourselves project. Kenny Freistat, a carpenter extraordinaire, answered my newspaper ad offering free rent in exchange for carpenter services. When I interviewed Kenny, I asked him, "Have you ever done a major remodel on a house?"

"I'm a journeyman carpenter, trained in the Midwest by a master craftsman who taught me a 10th of what he knew—but it's ten times more than what most of the California hot dogs know. Those guys out here aren't interested in quality, just quantity."

He got my attention. "I'll be doubling the size of this house," I told him. "The man I sold my last home to is a plumber, so we have worked out a trade. Can you run the rest of the project?"

"Sure." He was very confident.

The deal was made, and he moved his family into one of our apartments by the beach. The first day on the job, Kenny asked, "Who's going to do the drywall?"

"We are," I answered.

"Have you ever done drywall?"

"No, but I thought you could teach me." I had never even taken a shop class in school, but I had been doing a lot of the minor repairs on the rental properties I owned. And, for some reason, I thought I could build a house.

As it turned out, there was more to learn than I realized. One thing that building project taught me was the importance of sequential order. You can't put on the roof before the walls are up. Later, I found out that sequencing had been a weakness of mine, and building something tangible that I could see and touch did a lot to help me improve in this area. And as I know now, sequencing is *essential* to reading.

I brought in my father, Kathy's brother Mel, and another brother-in-law, none of whom could hammer a nail much better than I could, to join the team. Kenny taught us the tricks of the trade. A friend, Tommy Ellerbee, was a genius with tile, so he used his vacation time to help. My father-in-law brought in a friend who did the electrical work in exchange for a lobster dinner. I began to feel like Tom Sawyer persuading his friends to whitewash his fence.

After three months, we had a beautiful four-bedroom house that didn't even resemble the original.

Now I had the itch to dabble even more in real estate and remodeling. The few properties I had purchased were beginning to pay off. We would fix them up a little, sell them at a profit, and buy more.

Kenny became one of our best friends and is high on the list of rare books in my library. He still doesn't quite believe what I pulled him into with that first project. He loved to tell me, "Hey, John, you know there are labor laws — a slavemaster has to give his slaves some rest." He taught me much about construction skills, but some of my most memorable moments were on our back deck when Kenny, Kathy, and I would have lively discussions about philosophy, psychology, or politics. Kenny was continually giving me new books to read. Kathy read many of them, and I believe our son has read every book he ever gave me. Of course, I couldn't read any of them, but Kenny didn't know that and thought he was sharing something special with me.

Although Kenny and I continued to be involved in many building projects together, I soon learned that he wanted to get out of the building trades.

One day I said, "Well, what *do* you want to do, Kenny?"

"Go to college," he replied. "I want to use my brain."

Wow! Even though he used his brain every day as a carpenter, I knew what he meant.

"Okay, Kenny. You help me with my building projects and I'll help you go to college."

We both kept our bargain. It took him six years, but he graduated with a degree in creative writing from Long Beach State University. Today, Kenny laughs when he thinks of all those books he gave me to read.

KATHY CALLS OUR first seven years of marriage "the honeymoon years." We loved each other, the children were healthy and happy, and my career seemed secure. We were acquiring the trinkets of success. The world was squeezing us into its mold, however, and we didn't realize how we were being shaped.

WHEN OUR CHILDREN started catechism classes, we began courses in Parent Effectiveness Training, workshops in personal enrichment, and other self-help courses that were popular at the time. At first, some of the them, like Marriage Encounter, were very useful. However, we soon found ourselves accepting more and more humanistic ways of thinking.

In one of the groups Kathy and I attended, a book was passed around and everyone took turns reading. I said with great disdain, "I don't want to read," and passed the book to the next person. We had been told to be completely open with our feelings, and for one of the first times in my life, I didn't make up some phony excuse like "I forgot my glasses." I felt comfortable with what I said, but Kathy was furious.

"You were arrogant," she said. "You acted like you were too good to read from the book. Do you realize that you made everyone very uncomfortable? John, you humiliated me in front of all of those people."

Encounter groups usually were fun and not embarrassing. I was attentive when others were speaking, trying to be effective in communicating and facilitating others to communicate. This time, however, Kathy was upset. But the truth was that I didn't want to read because I *couldn't*.

Kathy usually felt that she had to explain my actions, to complete my sentences, to fill in my blanks. What she really wanted desperately to tell people was that I wasn't a jerk. She loved me and was usually very patient; but these groups and their sensitivity training were bringing out the worst in both of us.

Those second seven years were what Kathy called "the dark years." She said that the workshops and courses made her begin to question her basic beliefs. Sin and evil were irrelevant because we were told that if something felt good, and no one else was hurt, then it was okay. Everything was based on self-love and self-fulfillment. All the emphasis was on looking out for number one. Finally, when one of the workshops became blatantly sexual and open marriage and partner exchange was discussed, we knew we were steaming into dangerous waters.

Kathy said, "I want us to be who we were. We're heading down the wrong path." We were becoming trapped in spiritual darkness. We dropped the classes that were eroding our values; but tension continued to grow in our marriage.

The demands of a growing real estate business required more paper transactions. I couldn't write anything without Kathy, but she couldn't write exactly the way I wanted, nor could I express exactly the way I was thinking. It was much like a person who has suffered a stroke and can't push out the words he has hidden in his mind.

Kathy never taught me to read for the same reason a wise man doesn't try to teach his wife to drive a car. It can wreak havoc on even the best love relationships. However, we had a subconscious literacy program going on at home, with Kathy pronouncing words, correcting my grammar, and giving me word definitions on request. Her continual contributions to my growing vocabulary and language use were tremendous.

One night while we were recalling college capers, I told her about the time I had obtained the keys to the file cabinets that held tests, crawled along the ledge to the professor's office, climbed in the window, and copied the test answers. I was laughing when I told her, but Kathy said, "John, I don't think that's funny. I can't believe you would do such a dishonest thing."

Little by little, she was learning about the desperate behavior of an illiterate person.

In the 1960s, a white novelist, John Griffin, wrote an award-winning book titled *Black Like Me*. Griffin had taken a series of medical treatments to temporarily change his skin color to black, and then for several weeks he hitchhiked, walked, and rode buses through the deep South. The discrimination was so cruel that his scathing indictment of our society shocked American consciences. This is what he wrote in his introduction:

"The Negro. The South. These are details. The real story is the universal one of men who destroy the souls and bodies of other men for reasons neither really understands. It is the story of the persecuted, the defrauded, the feared and detested. I could have been a Jew in Nazi Germany, a Mexican in a number of states, or a member of any 'inferior' group. Only the details would have differed. The story would be the same.

"It traces the changes that occur to heart and body and intelligence when a so-called first-class citizen is cast on the junk heap of second-class citizenship."

When I was teaching school, I heard people talking about that book. I realized that I, too, was a second-class citizen. All I had to do was to look around at where the illiterates were and what people thought about them.

I'm not going to disclose my true identity and be tossed on that junk heap.

AS I BEGAN to buy more real estate, do more remodeling and selling, and turn more profits, my financial ambitions and independence were being realized. Even though I loved the ideals of teaching, I was frustrated with the gap between the ideals and the reality of the public school system. In 1977 I asked and was granted a year's leave of absence from teaching. That year I made $240,000. My salary at El Camino High the previous year had been $23,000 and I was dubbed "The Teacher with the Midas Touch."

My request for a second year's leave of absence was refused, so it seemed that I was destined to pursue real estate development. This was a difficult decision for Kathy. She liked being married to a teacher, with all the fringe benefits that accompanied that profession.

It was a lifestyle she enjoyed. Why would I leave it?

To me, it was like playing Monopoly every day. I took real estate seriously, as I did any game — only the big difference was that this money wasn't fake.

Fear of poverty was a motivating factor in my almost obsessive desire to achieve financial security. However, there was another more powerful force behind my drive, and that was to be looked upon as successful. Society seemed to have one yardstick for measuring success — money. An artist, scientist, or humanitarian might receive an occasional perfunctory good word, and sometimes the person who radiated a certain spiritual quality would be given a high rating. But if you had money you were on top of the ladder!

If you had money, you were smart because only smart people make money. With that false thinking, I coined my tacit battle cry: I am smart!

I began to purchase property like the average person might buy a new pair of shoes. On more than one occasion, I would drive past a place, take a look at it, and get a feeling that it was right for me. I knew what I was willing to pay for it and had some idea what I intended to do with it, so I would contact the owner and within days have a new piece of property or an apartment building. As inflation pushed prices upward, I would sell and acquire more. Early in the game I brought in Kathy's brother, Mel. He was bright, literate, trustworthy, and my best friend. He became my partner, and we continued to buy.

When we purchased rentals, we managed them ourselves. When we bought houses and condos, we did all the work for the face-lifts. When we bought land, we subdivided it. I was rapidly believing that making money in real estate came naturally to me. It must have had something to do with the way my mind works: I wasn't impressed by differences in the number of zeros in a figure. As a result, it took no more consideration for me to make a million-dollar deal than to make a thousand-dollar deal. Someone mentioned that I must have read Norman Vincent Peale because of my entrepreneurial positive attitude. "Sure," I'd say with a grin.

What started with a handshake and a 50/50 partnership with Mel became Mencor Enterprises. With inflation running rampant in those days, the company was exploding. Before long, it became the parent company of five subsidiaries: White Water Realty; Interior Design and Marketing Systems; Mencor Planning and Developers; Mencor Realty and Builders; and Shore Construction Company. It was one of the fastest growing development companies in North San Diego County. Mencor signs were springing up like dandelions after the rain as new construction began in many locations.

We brought many relatives into the company. Even my father was part of this flourishing business. Together we created our own microcosm, our own little world peopled by flawed, imperfect humans. For a time we accomplished our agreements with just a handshake. At a certain level, however, people stop appreciating handshakes and want written contracts. We moved out of the world of honorable gestures into the world of the literate. Not that there is anything dishonorable about the literate world — I just happened to be a faking, frightened stranger in it.

Since I could read only an occasional word on a document that crossed my desk, I had to rely on intuition and every trick I knew. As the president of the corporation, I handled things my way for a while.

After a time, however, our family-centered environment was disrupted. The aggressiveness I had developed for sheer survival in the literate world had become ingrained behavior. The problems of fast growth and management consumed me and presented a whole new set of problems for my illiteracy.

Building condos and apartments, putting together limited partnerships, hiring work crews, and coping with city and county regulations were immense challenges, but I dove into them like the man without a life jacket who had to swim or drown. I loved to build. I wanted to see beautiful, tangible results and draw the best people around me to ride that magic carpet to the land of gold and silver.

For some time, we looked good. We were growing and making money. But I was gone from home a lot and our family life was fragmented. *This will only be for a time*, I rationalized.

I found a piece of property high on a hill overlooking the city of Oceanside with a view of the ocean beyond, and I built our dream home, putting into that house everything I thought Kathy and the children would love.

That second seven-year period of our marriage was one of soaring income and business expansion that grew like an adolescent boy pumped full of vitamins. Yet something was missing. We were like the shell of a luxury liner, empty inside and steaming through the fog toward an iceberg.

Someone needed to sound a warning before we went aground or capsized.

We can make plans, but the final
outcome is in God's hands.
　　　　　— Proverbs 16:11

CHAPTER 11

The Walls Come Tumbling Down

WHAT BEGAN AS A SIMPLE errand to get a permit for renovating a house turned into a bitter reminder of everything that was wrong with my life. On a bright spring morning, with Pacific breezes buoying my spirits, I pulled up to the Oceanside City Hall, which was housed in a storefront behind an old shopping center. The planning department was familiar territory and should have held no risk for me; but when I pushed open the door, the muscles in my back and neck automatically tightened.

All my senses went on alert. This was enemy territory, which was any place people might expect me to read.

The signs pointing to the fire department, city engineer, and other offices meant nothing to me, but I knew my destination; I had bluffed my way through the planning department often enough to feel almost confident. As I approached the counter, I breathed easier because Jimmy, a former high school student of mine, was working the desk.

Jimmy's a pushover. I can easily manipulate him to fill out the forms.

"Morning, Jimmy."

"Hi, Mr. Corcoran. What can we do for you today?" His voice was quiet and controlled, just like I remembered.

"Here's what I'm trying to accomplish with a rental house," I said, leaning over the counter to sketch the changes I was planning and explaining the permits I would need.

Jimmy studied the sketch, looked up, and for the first time, I noticed how much he had matured. I couldn't help feeling a little twinge of pride for having been his teacher. He had been student body president and a tough, scrappy guard on the football team. Now he was an adult, earning a living, raising a family, making a start on a career. True, he was becoming a bureaucrat, but he was genuinely eager to help and be patient with those of us who have little tolerance of bureaucracy. I wanted to tell him how proud I was of him for what he had achieved. But I never got the chance.

After studying the sketch for an unusually long time, he looked up and said, "I'm afraid this isn't good enough, Mr. Corcoran."

My defense mechanism sounded an alert.

"What do you mean, not good enough?"

"I can't accept this. We have new regulations now. To get a permit for work like this, you have to fill out about three forms." He reached under the counter and began pulling out sheets of paper.

From sports, I had learned that the best offense is often a good defense. My first move was to attack.

"What on earth are you talking about, Jimmy?" I fumed. "I've never had to fill out these forms before. I don't have time for this. Just write the permit and let me get out of here."

His voice was controlled. He seemed to grow another inch when he said, "I know you've done things like this before without filling out the forms, Mr. Corcoran, but regulations have changed."

"What regulations? I don't know anything about new regulations." I was still on the attack but could feel my position starting to slip.

He turned and pulled a thick loose-leaf binder from a counter behind him. He flipped the binder around to me and pointed to a row of words.

"See for yourself," he said, with just a trace of bureaucratic smugness.

I was caught, but I had been in traps before and knew how to escape. I groped in my pockets, and then said with a grin, "Must have left my glasses at home. I can't read that size type without them. Just read it to me."

Jimmy turned the binder sideways, so we both could see the words. He recited slowly, "No property owner shall construct or cause to be constructed." The rules were all there.

As he read, my mind raced. I didn't want to take his stupid forms home for Kathy to fill out, then make another trip back. I just wanted to pay my fee, get the permit, and go to work. But an overachiever-turned-bureaucrat was standing in my way.

This kid, who just a few years ago was asking me permission to go to the bathroom, is brandishing all these papers to keep me from getting what I want. It isn't fair. I was starting to get angry, but it was an anger rooted in my own frustrations.

For 15 minutes, we squabbled over the regulations like two lawyers debating the death penalty. I was losing my case. My chances of getting the permit started to dim, and I could see another day wasted because I couldn't fill out a form.

However, I had another defensive ploy: pity.

I stepped back from the counter and raised my hands in mock surrender. "Okay, okay, Jimmy, you win. Oceanside's a big town now, and we have to do things in a big town way. But have pity on me, won't you? Don't make me run home to get my glasses, plow through these forms, then run back here again. Couldn't you just fill them out for me, just this once? I'll go over to the cashier's window and pay for the permit and by the time I'm back, you should have the paperwork done, okay?"

Jimmy took the forms and gave me a look of contempt. "You always have to have things your own way, don't you, Mr. Corcoran?" he said. He bent over the counter and started writing.

I almost spoke but stopped myself. I couldn't say what I wanted because that would mean revealing my secret. Instead, I went to the cashier and paid with a check, using the cheat sheet I carried with words written beside the numbers, then returned to pick up my permit.

"Thanks, Jimmy," I said, feeling ashamed of myself. "I really appreciate this."

"It's not Jimmy any more. People call me Jim." With that, he walked away. No smile. No friendly good-bye.

I went to the car, got in, and just sat, gripping the steering wheel with both hands. Shame, frustration, and fury were all growing and expanding inside me, like steam in a volcano.

No, this isn't what I wanted. I didn't need to have it my way, Jimmy. This time, I wanted to have it your way because I respect you, I admire what you're doing with your life. I wanted to fill out your darned forms, just as you asked, but I couldn't fill them out. And I can't even tell you the reason.

I had never felt so profoundly sad in my entire 40 years. Not because I couldn't fill out a few forms, but because I couldn't have an honest, natural association with a young man I liked. I had to lie and argue and manipulate, making both of us feel smaller.

How many times since grade school had I done something like this? How many friendships had I sabotaged? How many people had I alienated? How many times had I turned an opportunity for a real relationship into an ugly situation where no one could win? Too many times.

I suddenly found myself in the worst kind of midlife crisis. That day I came to realize how much of life I had lost simply because I couldn't read the words on a page. As I drove mechanically out of the parking lot toward home, I fought the numbing realization that for the same reason, more of life would elude me in the years ahead. Years lost, opportunities wasted, relationships destroyed — never to be recovered.

A boy named Jimmy never got to know me. A man named Jim probably never would either.

In the late 1970s and early 1980s, our business continued to flourish like a well-fertilized weed. My father was my silent partner; his specific job was to collect the rents from over 100 units we owned. But more important, he listened to my triumphs and challenges and encouraged me every day. He was proud of me, which made up for all the times he had to apologize for my bad behavior or persuade the principal to allow me back in school. He watched every play, as he had many times at my athletic games, cheered when I scored, but never booed when I fumbled. Every night I thanked God for him and his unwavering belief in me. It carried me through many crises to come.

The prime rate was creeping up, and that didn't bode well for our future. Each soaring point added to the interest on bank loans, and American business was seeing its growth potential threatened. Mencor had growing assets, an in-house attorney and CPA, bookkeepers and secretaries to handle the literate world. I thought I had all the bases covered, but I saw my empire beginning to tremble.

As we grew and added more personnel, some of our original enthusiasm began to sink into the mire of petty jealousies.

"John, I'm really cramped in this office. I need more room."

"I really need a larger desk."

"I prefer a room with a window that faces the ocean."

As president of the company, I knew those status issues were important for morale, but all I could think about was production and the bottom line. I gave my space to Mel, but immediately other vice presidents wondered why he got my office. So we did some quick juggling to make everyone fairly content and encouraged each person to contribute his or her expertise to our rapidly growing land development corporation.

All of this may seem superficial, but the constant bickering implied that I was doing something wrong. I wanted the best people around me and thought we would all share in the fruits of our labors if they would just follow this Pied Piper teacher with a Midas touch. However, interoffice rivalries continued to fester beneath the surface.

Our business was blessed with the arrival of Andrew Lo, a man who became a partner and friend. He came with much-needed capital from his Guam-based company, American Investments Incorporated. With millions of dollars of fresh capital investment, we could ride through the inevitable recession, regardless of its severity. We had land, capital, and the skills to build. Mencor was safe — I thought.

But along with Andy came new problems. It was necessary to reorganize, and in the shuffle Mel and Andy became equals. Mel wasn't too happy about that, and new power plays emerged. There was no overt antagonism, but a cancer was growing inside while everyone smiled, jogged, and ate health foods. By now, the infighting had gone beyond who would get the biggest office or wall-to-wall carpeting. People had become interested in positions on the board; they wanted to know what the guy next door was getting; they wanted day-to-day reports on where they stood; and each one wanted to stand with me on top of the ladder.

The problems were manageable, and I still believed the ship was solid. As long as I could use the literate skills of my employees, I knew I could sail the stormy seas.

The recession worsened. American Investments was losing confidence in America's economy and began to reevaluate its participation with us. We had to have their continuing financial support to survive. Our income was dwindling, but our overhead remained the same. We began to cut the fat. We started letting people go, and a quiet panic began to move through the company. *Who would be next?* We sold one of our computers. Bills began to stack up on my desk.

In the early days of the recession, few creditors were willing to discount their accounts receivable. When I asked for these concessions they would say, "Who do you think you are? Where do you get off having that kind of nerve?"

I took their remarks as personal failure. But when the recession widened and many companies found themselves in the same position as ours, I found it easier to settle more accounts. I would go to a creditor, speculate about his cash flow, and then say, "I have a serious cash flow problem on this project. I still owe $100,000, and I have $60,000. That means everybody has to take a 40 percent discount. If you can't accept this offer, you may get nothing."

My brashness in these encounters was a result of economic reality and the need to survive even in the face of embarrassment. I also was obligated to discount some of our accounts receivable and take a complete loss on others. Many of our creditors were cooperative, and eventually three-fourths of our debts were settled. But the other one-fourth was still outstanding, and litigation began. The paper world of contracts and agreements was entangling us like the tentacles of an octopus.

When I was home in the evening, there would be a knock on the door and someone would deliver another notice of a lawsuit. Sometimes those messengers of doom would come as late as midnight. *Is there no place I can find peace?*

In trying to solve my problems, I ran up against the literate world every day. The literates went to the written word in their contracts, bringing in attorneys and legal documents that had numbers and dollar signs throughout the pages. Numbers were the only things I could understand — and those numbers were big.

Find a solution. I had to save my company and never pull back. One of the most difficult things I ever did was to put both feet on the floor each morning and take them to my office. The second most difficult was to put my key in the door and walk in. The demands were so great, I didn't have time to think about the pain. Creditors were calling and coming in daily to remind me that we were behind in our payments.

To me, the literate society represented the Nazis. When Germany conquered France, Britain stood alone against the German war machine. The choices were to surrender or fight. Churchill urged his people to make this "their finest hour." I also asked myself, Kathy, my family, and my partners for the same sacrifice. My wife stood by, but some ran, some watched, and some grinned. I gave my "blood, sweat, and tears" to win victory at all costs. The battle of an illiterate against the literate world bombarded me day and night.

Humility had never been one of my better qualities, but I experienced its effects as I trudged from creditor to creditor, pleading for understanding. On more than one occasion I cried, and it wasn't the young Johnny playacting. Some listened; some showed compassion. Some made deals; others didn't. I had built a little empire on the *spirit* of the law, but I had to answer to the *letter* of the law.

Of course there were responses to be made, and I poured out my heart in the letters to creditors I had done business with for years, as I dictated copious pages to secretaries during the day and to Kathy at night.

One letter I sent to the president of a company, said:

"Good credit is the lifeblood of any business, and especially true of the development and building industry. I have worked hard to rebuild and restore credit, and I strongly feel next year I will show some black ink."

I put up our dream home as additional security for a four-million-dollar construction loan on 72 homes we were building. After explaining my plans to the creditor, I offered him the pink slip to my Mercedes and stated I would surrender it to him on demand.

In my opinion, one of the most serious problems facing our economic recovery (both personal and national) is the refusal to include the *spirit of the law* as well as the *letter of the law* in conducting our business affairs. The results of this behavior and thinking has created a nation of suers, and that translates into nonproductive and counterproductive behavior activities.

At one point, Mencor was being sued for $35 million. The figure was so overwhelming it almost lost its significance.

One day I staggered into the doctor's office, a bundle of frayed nerves. "Tension," he diagnosed, and gave me a book on stress to read. *Great...a book to read!*

WHEN KATHY WAS irritated with me (and I gave her many opportunities), she might say, "I'll help you with that letter," but then she would remember an errand and leave the house. She knew I was vulnerable, but she didn't realize that she was pouring salt on an open wound.

When I started to lose in one way, I'd create another game, a diversion, to pull me out. I didn't have the knowledge or skills to function in a literate society, so I fought like a trapped dog. I wanted to be petted, but I couldn't tell if someone was going to hand me a bone or kick me, so I bit a lot of the wrong people. I didn't like that about myself, but I seemed helpless to stop. I became self-centered and preoccupied with protecting my own world and image.

A lot of mud was dragged into the castle of our marriage as a result of my exterior arrogance, and Kathy spent time and energy cleaning up after my outbursts. "He knows better," she'd say apologetically. Many lesser wives would have deserted their husbands when times got rough. But Kathy pitched in and fought the battle with me and for me.

My family, however, was in serious upheaval. Kathy went back to work full-time as a nurse and John and Colleen were suffering from an absentee father, even when I was physically present. The madness of Mencor and my obsession with it was like a runaway train; it was derailing my relationships with the people I loved most.

One option was to fold my tent, cut my losses, admit defeat, and pull out. My partner and brother-in-law, Mel, did just that and brought a lawsuit against me after his departure. My best friend had become my enemy.

The aftershocks spread as Kathy's extended family and my extended family, who for many years had spent every major holiday together, went their separate ways. My dad and Mel, who had celebrated their same birthday together in the past, no longer did. Some cousins were estranged because they didn't understand why some family members weren't speaking to each other. Barbara, Kathy's younger sister, was the most neutral family member, and she consistently prayed that the stubborn Irish and volatile Portuguese would resolve their feud. Kathy was torn between her loyalty to her husband and to her brother.

It was during those stormy days that Barbara became more vocal about her beliefs and Kathy began to feel uneasy. "She's become a Jesus freak," Kathy would say. However, after another family scene when Barbara made herself "a fool for Christ," Kathy began to see her sister in a new light. "She let herself be humiliated, but she was powerful," Kathy said later. When everything started to fall apart, Barbara would hold hands with Kathy and other members of the family and pray.

Urged by her sister, Kathy began to attend a Bible study. "I can't remember any one big moment," Kathy said, "but I began to understand that a personal, not just a superficial, relationship with Jesus was what I was lacking. Barbara's prayers were certainly effective."

The wounds in the family were deep, but with time and forgiveness, the scars began to heal. Today those scars are barely visible. The family again celebrates the holidays together, and I know it was the prayers that Barbara initiated, and others continued, that started the reconciliation of our two families.

When the Mencor house of cards began to collapse, my silent partner, my father, had a stroke and became permanently silent. When I saw the athlete, the prize fighter, the feisty Irishman sitting limply in a wheelchair, I wondered, *What else can happen?* I never ceased talking to him about my problems, and just his nod and his smile encouraged me.

However, our business situation still looked grim, with no solution in sight. Declaring bankruptcy had been suggested many times, but to me that was unacceptable. I would not allow the literate world to give me another blank diploma.

Then came a vandalism episode involving our children. Unknown to us, for four years Colleen and young John had been joined by their cousins in what started as a prank but developed into a nasty holiday tradition. After our family Thanksgiving dinner, they left the house and went out and egged the house of a family who had been our longtime neighbors and friends.

When the kids were caught and the police called us, Kathy and I went into a state of shock. *Not our children! Our nice, middle-class kids? Unbelievable!* Colleen and John were too old to be sent to their rooms, but we certainly let them know how disappointed we were in them.

After I attempted to apologize on the phone for the kids' behavior, I could see that was not going to satisfy Mr. Wilson. He was too offended. A policeman called and told us that charges had been filed. I went to Mr. Wilson and asked him to drop the charges, because as head of our family, I would determine the penalty for my children's acts and make full restitution for any damages (which were less than $100).

He was adamant about pursuing with the prosecution. I reasoned, I appealed to his role as a father, but without success. Finally, John the Warrior crumbled. I dropped to my knees in the street in front of his house and begged, "In the name of Jesus Christ, forgive my family."

I never denied the right of Mr. Wilson and his family to be hurt or angry, but I felt my fatherhood was being threatened. There was no way they could know how the rest of my world was caving in on me.

The case was sent to the district attorney. A time was set for the trial, and although the district attorney did not want to pursue the case, Mr. Wilson wanted it prosecuted. I was not going to allow the state or my neighbor to dictate my role as a father. The economy might crash, business might fail, but it was my responsibility to discipline my children.

I was under fire everywhere. The literate lawyers were trying to put my business in a noose, and now, as I perceived, the literate authorities were challenging my parenthood.

After many months of anguish and several thousand dollars in legal fees, Mr. Wilson finally agreed to drop all charges. Several years later, when I was stranded on the highway with a flat tire, Mr. Wilson stopped to offer help. Peace, again, was established with old friends, and the power of mutual forgiveness melted our anger.

THE PERVASIVE FEAR of failure motivated me to press on. The words of those teachers who had said, "You'll never amount to anything," played in my ears. But I carried a resentment toward what I perceived as my prime enemy, the literate world. I know that isn't rational, since I was surrounded by those I loved who knew how to read and write, but the bitterness was always there. I believed that literate society, with its lawyers and affidavits, threatening letters, laws and subpoenas, depositions and liens, was out to force me into a dead end.

Our house on the hill was in jeopardy of foreclosure. This was the dream home that Kathy and I had designed and built, where we were going to live happily ever after. It was built for my family, and even though we were in great disruption, I refused to let anyone take it away from us. I was in a dark place, and the only way I could get out was through the law.

One lawyer who stuck with me, Wes Thompson, was stalwart, but he couldn't heal my tormented spirit. I knew I couldn't read and write, but I saw myself as a good communicator, and, in fact, if I had enough time, using metaphors and analogies I could communicate my thoughts. However, when it came to explaining to an attorney (while the meter was running), the relevant facts of a case in a logical and sequential manner, I found it difficult and frustrating. I began to have a new awareness that my oral language-processing skills were also deficient.

Even though those seven years were turbulent, Kathy calls them the years of "into the light" because she was attending Bible studies and reading her Bible daily. Raised in the Catholic church, I was used to tradition and ritual but had little knowledge of the Bible, except what I memorized in catechism or heard in Mass. Kathy was given a copy of a simplified version called *The Way,* and she began to read to me. I thought I knew what religion was—after all, I had attended church all my life. I had a little book of prayers, no bigger than the palm of my hand, that was given to me when I was in second grade. When I was especially despondent, I would pick it up and look at the pictures. One night, I took Kathy's Bible and put it under my pillow, thinking that perhaps God's wisdom would come right through the pages and show me the direction to go. I woke up with a stiff neck, but no resounding celestial voice that said, "John, here's what to do."

Sleep was almost an unknown luxury. Sometimes I would feel like I was suffocating under tons of papers, all containing words. Other times I was in a prison with a guard waving another lawsuit at me. *Where can I go? Who can help me?*

Kathy was not as uptight as I was. When she read her Bible, she seemed to find a calm in the midst of our storm. That book may have contained answers for her, but if I couldn't read it, how could I understand it? Her faith was so simple, so trusting. *If only I could have that kind of faith.*

One night I began to pray in a way I had never prayed before. I prostrated myself on the floor and pleaded, begged, cried, for a miracle. This was more than just down on my knees — this was down as low as I could get. I was utterly helpless.

I don't know how long I prayed, but I knew, perhaps for the first time, that I was honestly speaking to Jesus. I asked His forgiveness for not having faith. As I poured out my heart to Him, I knew I had reached a turning point in my life. When morning came, there was a new confidence in my life. For the first time in years I woke up refreshed, as if I had slept all night, and I sincerely believed everything was going to be all right. I would do what I could to untangle my family and business problems, but in the end I knew it was God who was going to take care of us.

Our problems, however, still seemed unsurmountable. At one time I had employed 20 people just to do the paperwork necessary for my company. But one by one I had let them all go. Wrestling with lawsuits, family tensions, and business failures, I was confronting a monster I thought I had already conquered in my lifelong battle. But that monster, the literate society, was now beating me to the ground.

During that time, the issue of illiteracy was being spotlighted for the first time in the national media — first by Barbara Bush, then by special programs on television. When I saw a public service announcement on ABC in which a father tries to read to his daughter, I wondered who wrote the script. They must have had me in mind! I felt my personal secret would soon be exposed, and the "literate society monster" would have me down for the final count.

One day I was in a grocery store and heard someone talking about the Carlsbad library literacy program. *Maybe someone can help me*, I thought. When I got home, I called the library and asked, "Do you have a literacy program?" Even then, I wondered if the librarian would question my inquiry. She told me where to find the Carlsbad Adult Learning Center.

A few weeks later, on a hot August day, I left home dressed in a suit and tie, looking for all the world like a hotshot businessman, and drove to a small, inconspicuous office in the next town. I was told the sign said, "Adult Learning Center of Carlsbad."

I didn't hear a voice from heaven, but as I walked in the door — 48 years old, frustrated, maybe even *desperate* — it was the beginning of my new life and the birth of a miracle.

*Since the Lord is directing our steps, why try to
understand everything that happens along the way?*
                                        — Proverbs 20:24

CHAPTER 12

Unmasking the Shame

I T WAS LATE ON A FRIDAY afternoon in August of 1986 when
I walked through the front door of the Adult Learning Center.
The office, located in a two-story professional building, was across
the street from a library. I had been to this building before and was
familiar with many of its occupants: a CPA, a real estate office, a
thrift and loan bank, an insurance agent, a travel agent, a dentist,
and an attorney. I thought it was ironic that I had successfully used
all of those professional services at one time or another, but "literacy"
could only be associated with failure and fear.

My visit to the literacy center was spontaneous. I had not made
an appointment and did not make it clear to the receptionist if I was
a prospective volunteer tutor or someone who had a reading problem
and was seeking information.

Anita, the receptionist, was seated at her desk. "May I help you?"
she asked with a smile. "I'm John Corcoran...I would like to see the
director of the literacy program," I said nervously. "Is this the right
place?" "Yes, it is. Lynda Jones is the coordinator, but she's out right
now. I expect her back in a few minutes."

"Well, it's Friday afernoon; she probably won't be back." I was already having second thoughts about being there; but I was also afraid that if I turned around and left, I would never come back.

"Please have a seat, Mr. Corcoran. She'll be back. May I get you a cup of coffee?"

Being on guard is second nature to functional illiterates. However, I had traveled so many roads and had so many experiences over the past 40 years of searching for a path to literacy, I thought maybe this was the time and place my journey would end.

Can they really teach someone like me to read?

Lynda Jones arrived, and I followed her into her office, feeling extremely apprehensive. She was a genuine, caring, sensitive person, however, and without any urging, I unmasked my shame. Not since I had revealed my secret to Kathy 20 years earlier had I told anyone my whole story.

"I'm here, Ms. Jones…well, I came here because…I know this must seem ridiculous, but…well, you see, I went through college and taught in high school…I have a business and no one knew…except Kathy…so I heard about this library literacy program, and what I thought might happen…there are so many papers in my business, you see…and it's so hard for me to hide anymore…what I'm trying to say is…*I want to learn to read.*"

Lynda was not surprised by my stumbling, awkward confession. She didn't look shocked, puzzled, or surprised.

"That's what we're here for, John, and please call me Lynda."

She was compassionate without being maudlin, professional without being rigid. I immediately felt safe with her and began to spill out more than four decades of accumulated frustration, starting with the dumb row and leading up to the current mountains of legal paperwork.

Later she would describe my torrent of words as sentences without periods. However, she didn't stop me at the time, even though I left long strings of words and thoughts suspended midair.

"John, you obviously have a large vocabulary as a result of your life's experiences, your traveling, and your upbringing in a well-educated family," Lynda said. "Although you may feel you are alone in this, there are many other adults like you."

Intellectually, her words were comforting. But emotionally I felt alone and didn't want to be put in a box and given a label like *closet illiterate.*

Lynda put a yellow tablet in front of me, handed me a pencil, and said, "Write down why you want to learn to read."

I called upon some memorized words from my years of copying. My throat was tight and tears started to blur my vision, but I grabbed the pencil and began to scribble. I tried to write: "Learn to write a book about how it feels...earn to read better..." *What did I mean, "better"? I couldn't read.* I stopped and slashed line after line through what I had written and now the tears began to run down my face.

That was the first time in my life I had attempted to write anything in another person's presence.

Lynda didn't seem the least bit surprised to see a big Irishman break down like someone who had experienced a death in the family. Raw emotions, suppressed for years, began to surface. In her years as director of the literacy center, she had seen many reactions from adult learners. She told me about one learner who had been through years of remedial reading, yet when he read aloud, it was complete gibberish. The tutor discovered his problem: He had never learned to read from left to right. Another learner was given a newspaper but couldn't make any sense out of the context, because she read it like a book. Instead of reading down a column, she would read across the page.

"Learners are like Swiss cheese," Lynda explained. "There are holes in their language comprehension. To those of us who have no trouble learning, it is difficult to understand where those holes are."

For instance, I could read the word *exit* when it was over a door, but put that same word into a sentence and I couldn't decode it. When it came to the words *push* or *pull* on a door, I didn't even try to read them because they were too similar. It was more expedient for me to use trial and error.

"I have just the right person for you, John. However, she is on vacation until September 1. I don't want you to wait a month to start, but I think she would be the right tutor for you," Lynda explained.

I have waited for over 40 years; another month won't make a difference... if I don't lose my nerve.

MY TUTOR WAS Eleanor Condit, and the first time I met her was at the Carlsbad library. This white-haired lady—who had less than 20 hours of training at the time—would turn out to be the second-grade teacher I never had. She was bright, had a sense of humor, and loved the English language. I found out that she had gone to Vassar for a year, and then left college to raise five children. For ten years she went to night school to get her college degree. She loved to read, and her enthusiasm was contagious.

She may have been small, but she kept me in line like no teacher ever had. She was a woman with determination and patience; those two characteristics were critical in the first 30 days. I believe she was another miracle God provided at a time when a weaker person would have given up on me.

We were assigned an empty office in the fire station next door to the literacy center. It was quiet in the evening, with no distractions. At first, she just let me talk and vent my frustrations. Then she brought out some books for learning adults. She would read to me, tracing the sentences with her finger as I looked on. The books were in a series called Sound Out, and were not like second-grade texts, but contained stories that would appeal to adults.

"Now, John, you read this page, paying attention to the vowels," Eleanor would say.

She began with one-syllable words, and I would try to sound them out. I had great difficulty distinguishing those sounds, particularly *i* and *e*. Sometimes my frustration would be so great I couldn't continue, but I would go home and work on *A-E-I-O-U*. Slowly, they began to emerge as letters that were on the page, not as Chinese characters on the front of a laundry ticket.

One time when Eleanor was drilling me in phonics, a fireman, a former student of mine, walked by and saw us. He waved and said, "Hi, Mr. Corcoran." I waved back and hoped he thought I was tutoring Eleanor.

As Eleanor continued to work with me, she would bring in magazines, like *Time* or *U.S. News & World Report*, and read current events or political stories. Then I would try to read them back to her. She also would read poetry to me, or even Shakespeare, just to let me hear the beauty of language.

We watched a seven-part TV series on the history of the English language. Being a history buff myself, this made language come alive for me. I really understood that language was simply the process of naming things.

One day she said, "John, why don't you start a journal? Just write down your thoughts. Don't worry about spelling or grammar; write whatever you want. It's nothing I need to see."

Many days I would get up at four in the morning and write for hours. As I shared my journal with Eleanor and asked her to correct my spelling, she tried to figure out the sequence in my disjointed sentences. I was afraid of showing anyone else what I had written.

For years, when I needed something written, I would wait until the last minute and then say, "Kathy, I need this right now." When a husband or a wife is the enabler, they have a certain power. At times I wondered if Kathy enjoyed the power she had because I couldn't read. A relationship has to be strong to withstand a drastic change in the one you love.

One evening I said to Eleanor, "You're a great teacher. I wish I had you in elementary school."

"I'm a tutor, not a teacher," Eleanor said. "Because they come from schools that are curriculum-centered, former teachers are not always good tutors. If history is the subject, then the school year must go from Columbus to Lincoln, or whatever the required study is for that period. If a child goes through the textbook, he passes. Children are taught to adapt to the curriculum. Adults, on the other hand, are learner-centered. They want to read and write to help solve their problems, get a better job, learn how to read instructions, be able to read with their children. Everyone's reason is personal. In our volunteer programs, we have taught people who have been rejected by structured educational programs."

When I met Eleanor, I didn't know what a complete sentence was. I also thought, as do many functional illiterates, that people who write professionally sit down and just let the words flow. I had no idea professionals rewrite a work many times.

AFTER MONTHS OF tutoring, I remember saying one day, "You know, it's just as if I've been living in a place where I could never see the light of day, but now dawn is breaking! English is *not* a foreign language. It makes sense!"

Eleanor was like the ambulance driver arriving on a scene where a bruised and bleeding man is crying for help. She stopped the bleeding and got me breathing again.

I began to look at the words on a page and say, "Aha! I get it! There is a system!" I could read strange words, not just those I had memorized over the years. I even started to use a dictionary, which was a major breakthrough. At times I felt like shouting, *I can read... I can read... I can read!* But I couldn't come out with those words, except to Eleanor, Lynda, and Kathy... the three important women who had known me before.

When I went to the literacy center I began to see many adults who just seemed to float in and then disappear, but there were others who tenaciously stayed to learn. Between 80 to 100 people each month were tutored by volunteers out of that small office. Forty-seven percent were high school graduates who had been passed from grade to grade, as I had been.

Eleanor said, "If we can help any of them, we've done something."

MY BELOVED FATHER died five months after I began learning to read. He had always loved me, but never knew all the years he had watched me grow, then worked with me in Mencor, that I was illiterate. I'm grateful that he died without knowing because I believe he might have blamed himself.

Mother began to understand my secret when she was almost 80 years old. She heard I was going to the literacy center and later began to find out about the extent of my illiteracy when the articles and interviews appeared. "I simply couldn't believe it," she said later. "John always took care of everything, and after my husband died, he took such good care of me. I was so shocked when I found out! I don't know how he did it."

I know that it saddened her to find out how I had suffered. She said to Kathy several times, "Where was I? How did I miss it?" But it also clarified for her the reasons for some of my childhood behavior and adult attitudes.

As I was learning to read, our business continued in a different form. Legal entanglements take years to unravel, but I was not going to call it quits. I continued to do some building, which helped pull us out of the real estate doldrums in the subsequent years.

IN THE SUMMER of 1986, when I began to learn to read, the San Diego Council on Literacy was founded to coordinate literacy efforts in the county. I believe this group, which is a network of literacy groups working together, is a flagship organization the rest of the country could follow. Ironically, it was because of the council that I was trapped into making the most important speech of my life.

One day after working with Eleanor for 13 months on my basic skills, Lynda said, "John, you have an unusual story. Would you like to share it with an audience of about 200 professional people, officers of companies, and community leaders?"

"Absolutely not," I replied, not too graciously.

What would my family think? What about my former students... my coworkers?

However, my joy of becoming a new reader was so great that I wanted to tell others about this miracle. I also realized that God might be giving me an opportunity to tell my story so that other new readers would feel free to share their stories. Besides, my whole style of living was taking calculated risks. *Why not?* I was strong and independent enough to take the consequences; but I didn't want to embarrass my family, the school district I had worked for, or my university.

I wrote a letter to my "Dearest Kathy," needing her understanding and support for the step I was about to take. After all, she had a large stake in this, since it would virtually be her revelation as well as mine.

After 22 years of marriage, I did not feel that Kathy really understood my struggle with literacy. She had witnessed me pursuing my dreams and accomplishing many of my goals. Consequently, she had difficulty understanding why illiteracy could be so traumatic. Hadn't I managed pretty well all those years?

I wanted Kathy to understand and to be my partner in this cause. With my newfound skills (and Eleanor's corrections), I wrote:

> The ghosts of my past scream out to me to join the war on illiteracy in America, to publicly speak and write about my personal experience, and the extent, causes, and suggested solutions to illiteracy in America. I cannot be free until I do my part to inform others. It is an ambitious and long-range project, but it is a goal that can be accomplished if we have the will.
>
> Kathy, I want you to actively join me on the front lines of the war against illiteracy in America. I believe that you would make an excellent spokesperson for the "cause," and I believe it could bring us even closer to each other, and we could have some fun along the way.

Your understanding of my problems with illiteracy is an important part of my healing and rehabilitation program.

Kathy agreed to come to my "coming out," but I don't think she was convinced my decision was wise. But it changed our lives, and she now calls the seven years that followed "the healing years."

THE SAN DIEGO Council on Literacy, together with the San Diego Chamber of Commerce, sponsored the Executive Breakfast, which was attended by heads of many companies. I was prepared with my speech, but I wasn't prepared for the repercussions.

Nothing on the program indicated that I was an adult learner or that this was my testimony. I was introduced as a former high school teacher turned builder-developer. It was a prestigious gathering; but in spite of my anxiety, I was determined to do my best. Jim Duffy, ABC president of communications, the keynote speaker, was to follow me.

A sophisticated group like that would not have tolerated a speaker who read his speech, but I faced them with 11 pages of typewritten script, carefully edited by Eleanor, who sat in the audience along with Lynda Jones. Kathy was at the speaker's table with me, as nervous as I was. I sat next to Mrs. Helen Copley, owner of Copley newspapers, and a remarkable woman who has made a big commitment to the literacy movement.

What has Lynda Jones gotten me into?

Soon after I began, I realized the room was as quiet as a cathedral. I picked up my papers and read much of the story that has been chronicled in previous chapters.

Yes, I am a graduate of a university, with a bachelor's degree in education and business administration. I have completed over 90 additional graduate hours in education, economics, and sociology at more than four major universities. I have experienced a continuing education in my professional careers as a developer, builder, and educator. I attended school 35 years. Half of those years I was a professional educator. It may be incredible or shocking to some, but it is undisputable that in acquiring these experiences, I could not read a textbook or write the answer to an essay question.

This is the first public acknowledgment that I have ever made, that I have been a functional illiterate for almost 50 years.

I cannot explain why I had so much difficulty decoding written words. Somehow, I missed out in the early grades. I easily learned how to count money and make change when I was six years old, but I didn't know all the alphabet until I was 12, and, even then, I was not confident.

Some people in the audience had that furrowed-brow look that said, "He's got to be kidding. How did he get through college and teach high school?" However, this group was more open than others, since they were concerned with the problem of illiteracy in America. It was a great dress rehearsal for what was to happen in the next few years.

Before I finished, I pulled out a poem I had written. It was the expression of the submerged feelings of a lifetime.

NATIVE ALIEN

Native Alien here from there,
You can be found everywhere,
Going though the motions,
Showing your emotions.

Oh! Native Alien, you are lame,
And literate society plays its games.
They still keep looking for someone to blame.
Isn't that the shame?
Don't they have any ideas of our pain?
It seems so plain,
But they keep looking for someone to blame,
What a national shame.

They give us our promotions,
And put us though the motions.

Bluebirds here, Redbirds there,
And now we have Jailbirds everywhere.

Oh! How we tried.
Oh! How we cried.
We were just past five,
And how we had to hide.
Oh! How we had to hide.
Oh! How they stole our pride.
Oh! How they lied.

Native Alien, here from there,
Native Alien everywhere.
Shame, shame, we can't read,

And how this nation bleeds.
But they still will not heed,
Why Johnny, the Native Alien,
Still can't read.

Oh! How we tried.
Oh! How many times has he died.
Literate society, you can't hide.
Oh! Literate society, how come you lie?
Scapegoat, cover up, alibi too.
Oh! Literate society shame on you.
Oh! Literate society you can't hide
Illiteracy statistics have your hide,
While you choke on your own pride.
Native Alien, he can't read.
It limits him, we concede,
But he has ideas, concepts, and theories too!
And that's the stuff of thought,
That you ought to concede to.

My mouth was so dry I could barely continue, but I kept my eyes glued to my speech and finished with a challenge.

I have taken the necessary steps and am making the commitments to personally overcome my lifelong handicap. I am a developing literate. I must pray and act to accomplish my goal — to become totally literate. I know I have much work ahead of me.

I invite you to actively join me on the front lines of the war against illiteracy in America. America must regain its competitive edge, and it cannot do that with an illiterate work force.

Your understanding of this illiteracy problem in America is an important part of the healing and rehabilitation of our country's most important natural resource, our people.

If you will lead, others will follow.

When I finished, I received a standing ovation. The kids in the smart row were welcoming me home from my long journey.

I looked at Kathy and saw her smiling with tears running down her face. I had broken through my grey cloud of silence, and the air was clear and invigorating.

That was the beginning of a road that took me from television studios to prisons, from universities to news interviews, and ultimately to the White House. I went from state to state, city to city, speaking about illiteracy. I had a lot to learn about the healing of the illiteracy scourge in America. Along the way, I would learn about the healing of the "teacher who couldn't read."

*This entire world of communication is cut off
from one in five Americans because they have
not learned to read.*

    — Barbara Prete and Gary E. Strong,
        Literate America Emerging

CHAPTER 13

A Cloud of Witnesses

A MOMENT OF TIME MAY BE a turning point in our lives, and the coming-out breakfast was one of those occasions. My story was written up in the *San Diego Tribune* and picked up by the news services, appearing in hundreds of papers across the nation. I began to receive calls from old friends, former students, and others I had not heard from in years. My story seemed to strike a nerve in the national conscience.

James Duffy, national spokesman for Project Literacy U.S., nominated me for Learner of the Month. As a result, I made a public service announcement on illiteracy over ABC and PBS; the networks received 25,000 calls for information. After it was aired, television appearances on major talk shows and an article in *Esquire* magazine, condensed in *Reader's Digest*, catapulted me into the spotlight.

One of my greatest challenges was the wave of emotion that flooded me as I recalled the past. It was embarrassing to stand before an audience and suddenly find my throat constrict and my voice quiver. There is something distinctly unsettling about a big man with greying hair choked up over his inability to read and write. A friend told me someone accused me of using emotion to generate a sympathetic response. They didn't realize that not teaching a child to read is a form of child abuse. It was the child in me crying out. At first, those childhood memories would attack me in unexpected waves, and sometimes at the most inopportune time. Thank God my family encouraged me during those times when I wondered why I had been led into this crusade.

AS THE MIRACLE of reading began to unfold for me, I believed God was leading me to greater boldness to help others realize that they, too, could break out of bondage.

Real estate building, development, and investment — as well as teaching — gave me the problem-solving, planning, and management skills to apply to this new endeavor: to bring the message of literacy, and some of the solutions, to as many people as possible. I don't believe that tired adage about not teaching an old dog new tricks. It's never too late to learn.

There will always be some who don't believe me. I was surprised that opposition would come from unusual sources. For instance, three weeks after the FBI had completed its investigation and filed a favorable report to the Senate for my appointment to the National Literacy Board, I was informed that the case had been reopened. An agent called me and said, "Mr. Corcoran, a letter saying that you are a liar and that you could read has turned up at the White House. Do you know why anyone would make an accusation like that?"

I was stunned. "There is no one on the face of the earth who has ever heard me read. Who is my accuser?" I asked. It was an anonymous letter.

It was an election year, but I was only a minor appointee. Who would want to destroy my credibility? Fortunately, my years in business had taught me to keep good files, and I had a clue about the writer's motives. I remembered a strange letter I had received from the *National Enquirer*. Someone had written the *Enquirer* about me, saying I was being investigated by the IRS for tax evasion, was hated in north San Diego County, and was a fraud because, the anonymous writer claimed, Corcoran can read. He gave names of people to contact, including a former employee, a subcontractor, and some competitors. The *Enquirer* wasn't interested in publishing the story, but somehow they had obtained my address and sent me a copy of the proposal.

I sent the entire document to the FBI. "I think I know who it is, but I'm only speculating," I said, giving them the name and phone number of a disgruntled former employee. He was just the type of personality who would have relished exposing me when I was a teacher if he had found out I couldn't read.

The FBI sent an agent to San Luis Obispo, where he spent the day questioning my teachers at a reading clinic where I had received over 100 hours of instruction. He asked, "Is there any possible way this guy could have been tricking you?"

The reading specialists knew my inadequacies well. "Why would John Corcoran come here and spend his time and money if he knew how to read? That's not even logical. We have diagnostic test results and case histories from thousands of people like John. We have treated thousands over the past 25 years who are highly functional. We know what those testing profiles look like before and after treatment. John's profile was typical of a highly intelligent person with severe auditory conceptual dysfunction. There is no way he could have known the profile pattern to fake!"

The FBI agent called and said, "No problem, John, you passed with flying colors."

That was one of several confrontations I would face for telling the truth about my illiteracy.

One of the bitterest blows came in my own backyard. It began when I was asked to speak to all of the Carlsbad school teachers. The superintendent, who had heard me speak at the annual conference of the Association of California School Administrators (where I had been enthusiastically greeted), issued an invitation for me to be the keynote speaker for his district. The date was already set when I received a call from the superintendent.

"John," he said, "we have a problem. A few teachers threaten to protest at the meeting because they say you're lying and you have been able to read all the time. Would you be willing to speak to the administrators only and prevent any embarrassment for the district and for me?"

I accepted his compromise and regrets, but I was hurt. The protestors probably were direct descendants of the teachers who put me in the dumb row and blamed me as a child for not trying hard enough. It was not only my integrity they discounted, but also that of the national volunteer literacy program, my tutor, and my wife.

A LOT OF PEOPLE with my disability are in jail, on welfare, standing in unemployment lines, or underemployed. But there I was, saying I had a college degree, had taught at a high school level for 17 years, and had built a large business, all without the reading skills of a second or third grader. I didn't know language was organized. Sentences, ideas that begin and reach a logical conclusion, speech patterns that start and end — all were foreign to me. Many times when I was making a long, involved analogy, I would hear, "Say what you mean." Sometimes when I would mispronounce a word or a name, someone would say, "Spell it." Language processing problems were constantly with me. I suspected that my oral and written language were connected, but never realized to what extent. As the pieces began to fit together I felt like an archaeologist discovering a new dig or fitting together my own Rosetta stone.

Why did it take me so long to go for help? A more important question is, why did it take society so long to offer us a safe place to go for help, where we could learn to read and achieve some dignity? As a child, I didn't know my problem. As I grew up, the charade I played was the only game I knew. Being an illiterate is like belonging to another culture. We feel as if we are members of some primitive tribe in a highly literate society. Since our oral language is also poor, the stigma is increased. For a long time, for instance, I couldn't pronounce my granddaughter's name. I called her Kaya. Her name is Kayla, but I couldn't hear that "l" to get the pronunciation right. As my reading skills improved, however, my oral ability also improved.

Someone has said, "Laugh and the whole world laughs with you; cry and you cry alone." That's not true. I began to hear about people whose hurts were as deep as mine, who needed an ambulance driver just like my tutor, Eleanor, to pick them up and take them to the reading hospital.

There are a cloud of witnesses out there, attesting to the fact that they are not stupid because they cannot read.

Entertainment shows dealing with illiteracy began to emerge from the scriptwriters' imaginations. One TV movie, *Bluffing It*, starring Dennis Weaver as a steelworker whose well-concealed illiteracy prevented him from career advancement, was broadcast in 1987, the same year I went public. That drama elicited 17,000 calls to the literacy hotline in seven days. American opinion began to stir over the need to do something about the hidden shame of illiteracy.

How could I have thought I was so alone?

WHEN NEW READERS begin to speak out and tell their stories, they send out powerful messages — some of hope, others of despair. Many tell about the consequences of the cycle of family illiteracy, closed doors for job opportunities, the descent into drugs and alcohol, prison and homelessness. Others are surprises; people who made it in business or professions, in spite of their illiteracy. All tell of the pain and anguish of this blight on society.

A senator's wife, Ann Mathias, said, "None of the teachers believed me. I was accused again and again of not doing my homework... I felt the only thing I had was my integrity, and to have it questioned struck at my very innards."[1]

Bruce Jenner, Olympic champion, said, "Dyslexia is a much misunderstood handicap, and probably no one misunderstands it more than the victim of it prior to diagnosis. When in school, I couldn't fathom why I was not capable of reading as eloquently and gracefully as others in the classroom. It was a tremendous source of discomfort and embarrassment when the teachers called upon me to read aloud."[2]

In the book *Literate America Emerging*, the authors gathered stories of new readers like myself. Gene said, "When I was in the seventh grade, I asked a teacher why I couldn't read, what I had to do. She said I was going through a phase, I asked how long this phase would last. She said a short time. I went back a year later, and she said the same thing. This lady was teaching in the school system until a year ago."

Gene was the president of a credit union, worked as a modification engineer for Caterpillar, and helped train Wells Fargo bank personnel. He said, "People I helped never knew I was illiterate." How did he do it? He carried a tape recorder and recorded directions, information, ideas. His wife helped him interpret memos or instructions. She was an avid reader and became his eyes. Tragically, his wife became blind and Gene knew he had to learn to read. She asked him in amazement, "Do you mean to tell me that since we were married you couldn't read?" His kids couldn't believe him, either, and asked him how he could have helped them with essays.

"They didn't know it took me a half hour to write a regular sentence with a dictionary. I'd stay up all night to read their homework. My ultimate goal then was to read *National Geographic* to understand what the pictures were about."[3]

In his superb book *Read with Me*, Walter Anderson tells how the power of reading transforms lives. One subject, Elaine Williams, was a high school graduate with a lifelong difficulty in reading. Her language-learning disability went unrecognized in every school she attended as a child and as an adolescent. She was stereotyped in second grade as the dummy and was a social outcast.

Elaine said, "Instead of turning into the class clown or class bully, I withdrew. My life became a living hell. In Sunday school I'd ask God to take my life. I thought about suicide, but I was too afraid."

Elaine was passed from grade to grade. Her parents were both readers and were told by the school authorities that there was no reason she couldn't learn to read. "They recommended that we go as a family to a youth guidance center. My parents had to listen each week to how rotten they were...so my disorder, unrecognized by the school system, affected my parents as well as me."

Fortunately, Elaine discovered a literacy program at her hometown library, where a sensitive and kind tutor spoke to her with respect and started her on the path to reading. She later got a job at the office for Literacy Volunteers of Massachusetts. Given a chance to talk to many students, she said, "There are so many misunderstandings. One is that students feel that they know less than they really do because of all their guilt. They think, *this is my fault!*"[4]

ROBERT MENDEZ IS a new friend who graduated from high school in 1967 yet couldn't read his diploma. He resigned himself to the idea that he would only get the lowest paying jobs. After the frustration of janitorial jobs, knowing he was capable of something better, he heard about the Laubach reading program on the radio. He said, "I knew what I needed, and the literacy council could give it to me — a friend who could teach me one on one, no classroom; someone I could relate to, someone who would help me get rid of the luggage of guilt I carried and my terrible feelings of inadequacy." He found that friend in a tutor who taught him to read.

"When I was a child, reading was painful, the one thing to avoid, the thing that I wanted to get away from. Words were my fear. If I walked into a room and saw a pen, paper, or books, I'd find five reasons to leave — and that's something that people who can read don't understand, that people who cannot read are intimidated by words and letters. To learn to read, we have to reprogram ourselves to see words as friends, not enemies."

Mendez was asked if there was any special moment he experienced after learning to read. He answered, "Yes, there was a moment: when I read Mickey Mouse's number book to my three-year-old. I started to cry, and he asked me, 'Daddy, this isn't such a sad book. Why are you crying?'"[5]

Linda, a new reader, wrote me a letter (with the help of her tutor in a library literacy program) and said, "It was encouraging to me to see you on TV and letting the world know that you overcame a secret you hid for years and a secret that we shared.

"Hearing you speak and expressing the emotions you felt, I am more determined to work even harder to reach my goals... I have three goals now: to learn to read better, to learn to read the Bible, and to learn to write letters. I am working on writing to you, one day, on my own."

Wilbert Rideau has been imprisoned since 1962 at the Louisiana State Penitentiary serving a life sentence. During that time, he has become a renowned journalist, author, and advocate of prison reform. In an interview with *Time*, he made some pointed statements. He said, "Public fear is out of control, so he (meaning Bill Clinton's crime package) has to put more police on the streets. Boot camps can help, but often they're just another feel-good device for punishing criminals. I'd like to see more efforts aimed at really improving people. Crime is a social problem, and education is the only real deterrent. Look at all of us in prison: We were all truants and dropouts, a failure of the education system. Look at your truancy problem, and you're looking at your future prisoners. Put the money there."[6]

For all of the successful emerging literates, there are millions who are left behind, caught in the world or underworld of crime and poverty. Can we save any of them? If the Good Shepherd searched for one lost sheep, isn't one more life saved from the junk heap worth our effort?

Jonathan Kozol, author of the landmark 1984 book *Illiterate America*, alerted our country to the seriousness and far-reaching effects of illiteracy. We appeared together on several television programs, and I respect his contribution in making Americans aware of our problem. He pointed out that the United States ranks 20th among 22 industrialized nations in literacy. What a high price in lost business productivity, ruined lives, and international embarrassment this scandal is causing!

I'm not so naive to believe that literacy is the complete answer to America's problems. We are beset by a sliding morality that is accelerating like an avalanche in the Sierras. However, engineers and geologists have discovered ways to dynamite snow masses and halt the destructive onslaught. In the same way, we have the means to slow the growth of illiteracy; to rescue some who are headed for prison, welfare, or unemployment lines; to enable the Word of God to be read; to give a sense of worth to the men, women, and children still trapped in the "dumb row." It's not too late.

IN 1988, I was invited to Washington, D.C., to participate in the most ambitious public service campaign television had undertaken: Project Literacy U.S., more commonly known as PLUS. First Lady Barbara Bush was at that meeting, and I had the opportunity to talk with her about our common concern: literacy in America. For Barbara Bush, the fight against illiteracy began years before when she discovered that her third son, Neil, couldn't read. After many years of special tutoring, he managed to overcome a severe reading disability, but his childhood battle left a lasting impression on his mother. When George Bush decided to run for president, she was convinced that she had a rare opportunity to make a difference in the lives of millions of Americans. She said, "Knowing that George was going to run for national office, I spent a whole summer thinking about what would help the most people possible. And it suddenly occurred to me that everything I worry about — things like teen-age pregnancies, the breakup of families, drugs, AIDS, the homeless — everything would be better if more people could read, write, and understand."[7]

She established the Barbara Bush Foundation for Family Literacy, a public, nonprofit organization that provides grants for programs all over the United States. Most of all, she provided hope that literacy programs could help, and that the most important place to start was in the family, with parents reading to their children and becoming aware of learning disabilities at an early stage.

Mrs. Bush became the inspiration for a homework assignment that I had not been able to complete in my sixth-grade class. Even though Mrs. Richardson had been one of my better teachers (and I had a preadolescent crush on her), she didn't teach me to read. When I was over 50 years old I wrote her this letter:

Mrs. Richardson
My 6th Grade Teacher
Wherever You Are

Dear Mrs. Richardson:

I am finally learning how to read and write, which has enabled me to complete my homework assignment, an essay entitled, "My Contemporary Hero."

I realize that I am 40 years late turning in this assignment; however, I hope you will accept my essay and realize that I was not lazy, but one of millions of children that have difficulties learning how to read and write.

Your acceptance of me was always important, because teachers are important people.

Sincerely,
John Corcoran

MY CONTEMPORARY HERO
by John Corcoran

Reading and writing skills managed to elude me for more than 40 years, although my reading skills have improved significantly in the last three years. My spelling and writing is still laborious and very time consuming.

For a long time I have hidden most of the pain and frustration related to my poor reading and writing skills. Finding words to express what I had stored up is now the driving force for my progress and commitment to a literate America.

Illiterates or functional illiterates in America are our most underutilized resources. The lack of an educated work force may well become a serious contributing factor in preventing America from competing effectively in the emerging global economy.

In recent years I have often heard that Americans have few contemporary heroes to emulate. I have many contemporary heroes. They are those people involved in the literacy movement. It is difficult to select just one person. My list of nominees includes the ever-growing number of people from the grassroots of America: It includes new readers, my volunteer tutor, Eleanor Condit, and our First Lady, Barbara Bush, who is our national spokesperson for literacy.

Literacy is as fundamental as free speech and a free press; it is the fundamental right of every citizen. Barbara Bush is a champion for that fundamental right and Barbara Bush is surely one of *my* contemporary heroes.

That school assignment took 40 years for me to complete. Mrs. Richardson, will you please give me a passing grade?

One of the hardest assignments I have had is to talk to teachers. It is a challenge to address dedicated, hardworking classroom teachers and tell them that we have failed to teach our children — all our children — how to read and write. I must place myself with them in this neglect. Together we must find ways to break the cycle of failure. The great confusion over effective reading instruction can and must be ended. We can no longer afford to waste our time and energy blaming, scapegoating, and manufacturing alibis.

Society, and particularly teachers, must be prepared to answer the following question positively: *Do you* believe every child's brain has the potential for literacy?

Unless a teacher has medical evidence that an individual child is incapable of learning to read and write, that teacher must believe in, encourage, and befriend every child in the class. Those children who have special problems must be given special help. We must dismantle some of the theories of how the brain is dysfunctional and seek the positive approaches that do not attempt to blame the child for slow learning.

For over 90 million adults — about 42 percent of the U.S. adult population — read is not a wonderful word. They are the people who have the lowest level of literacy, according to a nationwide study released by the Department of Education in 1993.[8] Those individuals appear to be the most at risk in our society, where literacy is a key to opportunity.

Here are some statistics that should give all of us a wake-up call:

- Twenty-one to 23 percent, or some 40 to 44 million of the 191 million adults in this country, are unable to manage a checking account, fill out a job application, read street signs, or read to their children.

- An additional 50 million adults, or 25 to 28 percent of the adult population, say they get a lot of help from family members or friends with everyday prose, documents, and simple literacy tasks. Those at this level are unable to succeed with tasks that call for low-level background knowledge.

- Twenty percent of those with the worst literacy skills have high school diplomas.

- One million students drop out of school each year, lacking reading, writing, and fundamental job skills.

- Each year businesses hire one million new workers who cannot read, write, or count. During the time it takes to teach them, their employers lose $25-30 billion in productivity.

- Employers spend $21 billion annually to teach basic reading, writing, and fundamental job skills. Currently, 30 percent of all large companies offer remedial education. Over the next decade, that figure will climb to 65 percent.

- Seventy percent of today's jobs require a ninth-grade reading level. "We have estimated that only about 25 percent of the adult population is highly literate," said Brenda Bell, vice president of marketing for the National Alliance of Business, a group of 3,000 businesses engaged in work force training and education issues.

- By the year 2000, most jobs will require at least two years of college education.[9]

Are there solutions to the grim statistics of illiteracy in America? Yes, there are. We only need to listen to those voices crying in the wilderness who have the answers many in the educational establishment refuse to hear. Offering calculators and computers, longer school days, or more special education classes to the millions of students who never learned basic reading skills is a travesty.

The only answer for *illiteracy* is *literacy*.

I think killing phonics was one of the greatest
causes of illiteracy in the country. —Dr. Seuss

CHAPTER 14

Phonics First

IN 1955, PHONICS ADVOCATE Rudolf Flesch wrote *Why Johnny Can't Read*. I was in high school that year, copying papers, cheating on tests, doing anything to get a passing grade. I knew I couldn't read. No one had to write a book about it. Twenty-five years after his first book, Flesch followed with *Why Johnny* Still *Can't Read*. Had anyone been listening?

When I began with my volunteer tutor, Eleanor, she endeavored to teach me phonetically. I learned the concept of decoding words, although my decoding skills were far from what they would become. Today, the subject of phonics-first in our American schools is still being debated and argued in academia. Meanwhile, according to the National Adult Literacy Survey done for the U.S. Department of Education, 93 million persons aged 16 or older demonstrate very low levels of literacy.[1]

Functionally illiterate adults were children once. Many are graduates of our educational system. Our society must presume that every child goes to school expecting to learn to read. If he doesn't, is it his fault? I believe the child is innocent and not to blame. And the school system bears at least 51 percent of the responsibility to teach every child to read.

Today's children continue to slide through the public school system, drop out, or enter the work force without enough skills to compete, while the illiteracy rates climb faster than the national debt.

Some voices have been crying in the wilderness for years, challenging prevalent educational methods and consequences. My friend, Dr. Patrick Groff, professor of education at San Diego State University, decided 25 years ago to enter the reading method debate with an open mind. If I had known Dr. Groff when I was teaching high school, he probably would have seen right through my "progressive" teaching as a method to disguise my own illiteracy. Now he and I are allies in this battle for a literate America.

In 1967 Dr. Groff, along with 24 other English professors and educators, were chosen to study how reading and writing were being taught, and the best methods to use. They spent a year in research at the University of Nebraska, with all of their expenses and salaries paid by the U.S. Department of Education. Those scholars produced volumes of evidence that verified the wisdom of phonics-first in the elementary grades.

What happened to that report? Dr. Groff told me, "As far as I know, those research findings of two dozen scholars over a period of a year, paid from government coffers, were never implemented. The reports were probably lost in the labyrinth of other projects which have been consigned to the shredders. If not, why weren't those suggestions spread to the institutions that design the teachers' curriculum?"

Who wants to kill phonics? And why?

Bob Sweet, another friend and president of the Right to Read Foundation in Washington, D.C., believes there is no reason for

America to have reading problems. He said, "We know what works: *intensive systematic phonics.*" As a former teacher and a deputy director of the National Institute of Education, Sweet stated, "Children taught to read using systematic phonics can usually read and understand at least as many words as they have in their spoken vocabulary by the end of the fourth grade."

When I was in the fourth grade, I was sitting in the circle of nonreaders who were tagged Buzzards. I wonder how many Buzzards are adult nonreaders today.

Michael Brunner is with the Office of Juvenile Justice and Delinquency Prevention in the U.S. Department of Justice. Brunner said, "Teachers are led to believe that it is not teaching methods that have failed, but students who cannot learn to read, or read well, because they are learning disabled."

How many students with the learning-disabilities label may be suffering from teaching disabilities? Here's a revealing report from Gallegos Elementary School in Tucson, Arizona:

In 1986, it had an enrollment of 623 students, 53% were Hispanic, 2% were African Americans, and 4% native Americans or Asian-American children. They were from low socio-economic families and many one-parent and unemployed parents. In many cases, both parents worked. Quite a few were on welfare. What is significant is that 46% of the intermediate students, all of whom had transferred to Gallegos, had been in Special Education, most classified as learning disabled. One year later, only four students remained in Special Education. What distinguished Gallegos Elementary School was the fact that it was the *only* school in the district using a phonics-based language arts reading program."[2]

English is a phonetic language, which is true of most of the romance languages; you analyze the parts and put them back together. Once you can decode words, you can make sense out of what is on the page. Chinese, however, is not an alphabetic or phonetic language. Inflection decides the difference in Chinese words, which is the reason those of us who do not know the language hear only its sing-song intonations without understanding any words.

I WAS TOLD about a seven-year-old child who was retained for two years in kindergarten. Her parents said she had an attention problem. She was asked to read the word *pan*, but she had never understood the relationship between the letters she saw and the sounds they made. One day she surprised her teacher by saying, "Oh, I get it. You do a little bit of this one, and a little bit of that one, and then you *smooth* them together."

Yes, that's it! That's how words work. But is that the way children in our public schools are being taught? Here are some of the methods being used today, with the abysmal results showing up in our illiteracy statistics.

THE WHOLE-LANGUAGE or whole-word approach (sometimes called *look-say, eclectic approach*, or *psycholinguistics*) urges children to omit, substitute, and add words in what they read. The advocates of this method insist that children supposedly learn to read simply "by reading," with no direct and systematic teaching of phonics necessary. For instance, if a child is reading a sentence and doesn't know a word, and he can't sound it out phonetically, he simply inserts whatever word seems to make sense in the context of the sentence. If the sentence reads, "I like carrots," but he doesn't recognize the last word, he might substitute something else. "I like cars." The sentence may make sense, but that is not what it says.

Children in whole-language classes are not always expected to understand the exact meanings the authors intended. As a new reader, I can only imagine how confused I would have been if my tutor had said, "Now, John, don't worry about the words you can't read, just skip over and say *blank*, or put in whatever word that you think makes sense." No telling what word I would have put in the blank. To me, this seems more like guessing than reading.

At one public elementary school, parents were concerned about their children's apparent inabilities to read and write. A special PTA meeting was called and a reading specialist presented a lecture on "A Balanced Whole Language Program." She explained how children are taught to read, write, and spell with this method. In conclusion, she added, "Phonics is only used when the child is ready — usually beginning in the third or fourth grade. Even then, we use phonics in a very limited practical way."

Perhaps some parents at that meeting believed this expert had the right answers. However, they should have been jolted out of their chairs when the special education teacher said, "You are very fortunate that this school has a high percentage of students enrolled in special education."

Why were so many students enrolled in special education? Could it possibly be because they didn't have a clue how to phonetically put together sounds and letters?

Jim Jacobson, a former educator who served under Secretary of Education William Bennett and later became a policy analyst under President Reagan, told the story about that PTA meeting and the puzzled parents who attended. "Experts agree that the whole-language approach can be useful after a child has been taught to read phonetically. However, without phonics first, whole language can create serious reading problems for many children."[3]

Serious enough, I might add, to be labeled "learning disabled."

A recent seven-year study at Bowman Gray School of Medicine and National Institute of Health stated that American schoolchildren with dyslexia were having their reading problems compounded by using the whole-language approach. The study found that teaching these children to read by recognizing whole words was not an adequate substitute for traditional phonics lessons. In this study, kindergartners were divided into three groups with three different types of instructions. By the third grade, the phonics group could read at significantly higher levels than their whole-language peers.

Dr. Groff said that in other countries the story is the same. In Bromley, England, the track record for nonphonetic methods of teaching was so bad that the school board would "no longer honor course work taken by its teachers in the whole-language approach... nor hire new teachers so trained."[4]

In the book *Gifts Differing*, Isabel Meyers says that all children will flounder in school if they don't learn the meanings of symbols for sounds and letters. Unfortunately, their failures may be blamed on low IQ or emotional difficulties. "Actually the failures... could all result from one omission. Nobody helped them, in the beginning, to learn the explicit meaning of the sound-symbols."[5]

WHAT A DIFFERENCE the meaning of sound-symbols, phonetic teaching, and a little extra time makes in learning. Imagine how the performance of students in the lower half of the class might improve if they just had a few more seconds or minutes to respond. A child needs to feel a sense of accomplishment, and if he consistently fails, or feels he is failing, discouragement may block his ability to learn and develop. Are children being given the time they need to succeed?

I know that feeling: *Why try? It's hopeless.*

When I was in grade school, phonetic teaching may have been used, but it went right over my head. However, Eleanor — with a great deal of patience — taught me to read using phonics.

Children who know their alphabet letters and find out that they stand for sounds can read as soon as they figure out the code. For some children, this is so easy they seem to teach themselves to read. They understand what it means when we say, "It's as simple as ABC."

IF YOU ARE reading this book, you undoubtedly are not conscious of phonics, nor do you stop to figure out how each word sounds. It's like riding a bicycle. We forget about the spills or how our dad held on while we were weaving down the sidewalk and trying to balance on those two skinny tires. We may have learned without any help, just trial and error and a few bruises. Once we learned, however, we never forgot. To some, reading may be as natural as breathing; but to others, it's like an asthmatic's desperate attempt to catch a breath.

If a child is to learn to read well, phonics-first proponents say he needs four main ingredients: *first*, phonics information and how to apply it to recognize words; *second*, familiarity with the meanings of words; *third*, a literal understanding of what the authors intended to convey; and *fourth*, a critical attitude toward what is read.

The rule of phonics is that a speech sound is spelled frequently by a certain letter (or cluster of letters), and in no other way. For example, the speech sounds *r-a-t,* in this order, are spelled *rat*. Children apply phonics rules to gain the approximate pronunciations of written words. After this, they usually can deduce the normal pronunciations.

If a child understands the individual letters in the word *rat*, then, as his skill grows in phonics application, he can quickly recognize letter clusters like *fat, cat, mat,* and so forth.

When a child can understand words, reading should become a joy. But when letters and words on a page make no sense, the restless, inattentive, troublemaking Johnny or Sue disrupts the entire class.

The famous old *McGuffey Readers*, considered by many educators today as antiquated, taught generations of children to learn to read with its phonics-based methods. However, at the turn of the century, progressive education, along with John Dewey as one of its famous champions, began to advance the whole-word method. In fact, the progressive teacher-educators warned phonics teachers that they would become mechanical taskmasters, driving pupils through parrotlike drills. Phonics was even condemned as dangerous to children before the age of eight or nine.

After 1967, an antiphonics movement began to grow again. It was claimed that teaching phonics is likely to do more harm than good, since it is impossible for children to identify the name of a word from the speech sounds that its letters represent. Some negative critics say that only a "little dab" of phonics is needed by children and that overemphasis on phonics interferes with a child's ability to comprehend what he learns. Research evidence does not support these erroneous comments about phonics, but they are found in many educational journals and books written for teachers.

TRADITION HAS A powerful grasp on some people's thinking. Even in the face of facts, some educators refuse to give up malpractice in reading instruction because it would be embarrassing to reveal that their methods are inadequate. Thus illiteracy statistics are blamed on everyone or everything — except teaching methods.

When I was teaching, the phonics or antiphonics debate was irrelevant to me. I taught the way I learned, and that was with oral language, films, stories, and common sense. Teachers still teach the way they learned, and most of them are being taught the whole-language recipe, with a pinch of phonics.

When reading educators discredit phonics, convinced that it is dated, unfashionable, or even obsolete, they pass on these ideas to the next group of teachers.

Many phonics opponents accuse the defenders of intensive phonics teaching as being conservative or right-wing. For instance, one reading professor told her professional colleagues, "Even though we might agree with a part of what they [phonics advocates] say, the association between phonics instruction and conservatism suppresses our saying so. In some circles, mentioning that you think a code-breaking approach to beginning reading might be appropriate for some children is tantamount to supporting John Birch."

Literacy is apolitical. It is criminal that partisan politics should enter the field of educating our children and adults. Teaching children to read is the most important objective educators have to accomplish. Reading is the prerequisite for everything else, not only in school, but in life itself. There should be no debate about that. We are fragmented and polarized into so many different camps that we have created an educational gridlock.

Many people seek power and influence over the minds or behavior of others, and one way is to make complex something that should be simple. Literacy is fundamental. Why should it be the property of liberal or conservative, Democrat or Republican?

I was recently asked why so many conservatives are advocates for phonics. I can't answer for others, but as a builder I know the single most important aspect of building a house is the foundation, the concrete and steel that keeps a house from falling down. Most builders, whether they are politically liberal or conservative, would agree. Phonics is the foundation for my literacy skills, and it has nothing to do with my political beliefs.

I would not be able to read, write, or spell today if I had not been taught to decode words phonetically. Without phonics, my electronic dictionary and thesaurus would be useless gadgets.

It's hard to blame dedicated teachers when their teacher training, union influence, and mandated district policies direct them away from phonetic teaching. But we still must hold them responsible for teaching children to read.

Some educators persist in telling us that a parent or nonprofessional shouldn't try to teach a child or adult to read. Come on now — this isn't performing brain surgery!

Some parents have the concern and sensitivity to discover their child's problem and take action. Here's one story a father told the Right to Read Foundation:

My daughter Renee is seven years old and a second grader. She attended a Montessori kindergarten, was taught reading with a phonics program, and was already beginning to read when she entered first grade.

As the year progressed I would sit down with Renee while she was reading, and I noticed that she was guessing at unfamiliar words, sometimes wildly guessing, instead of sounding them out.

At the beginning of Renee's second grade school year I was told that she had been placed in the lowest reading group. There was something seriously wrong, so I started to investigate. I discovered that Renee's school taught the whole-language method.

This father began to teach his daughter phonics at home, and after a couple of months, working with her two days a week, her reading had so improved that she could read the longest, most complicated words from her children's books, some adult books, and even an unabridged dictionary.

What would have happened to Renee if her father hadn't caught the school's inadequacy? This true story is typical of what is heard from hundreds of parents all across America.

I HAVE TRIED to emphasize the importance of phonetic teaching. My granddaughters learned to read with ease by the phonetic method taught in their Montessori preschool. But I must add that many children and adults, like myself, may need a more intense, basic phonics.

One day some time after I had revealed my four-decade handicap, I received a phone call from a lady who had read about me in the newspaper. She said she had an idea that could help me. I put my hand over the receiver and said to Kathy, "Another snake-oil salesperson." That cynical remark proved to be incorrect, for this lady was to introduce me to the missing piece.

My reading puzzle was about to fit together after being scattered for 50 years.

*I firmly believe that the problem of illiteracy can now
be tackled head-on by prevention. The key is the discovery
of the cause of reading problems.*
> —Dr. Steve Truch, director of
> *The Reading Foundation,* Calgary, Alberta

CHAPTER 15

The Missing Element

WHEN I WENT PUBLIC, I described myself not as dyslexic or learning disabled, but as illiterate because that is the way I saw myself. As I told my experiences in learning how to read, write, and spell, I began to suspect that I didn't have the entire solution to my language processing. Where was the elusive piece of the puzzle? My phonics training with Eleanor gave me the foundation I needed, but it was like a cake that fell flat. Something was missing.

A lot of snake-oil salespeople, as I irreverently called them, emerged to give me advice. One company offered me $20,000 to endorse a teaching tool they had developed. The money was tempting, but the product was questionable. A woman in L.A. was selling franchises for a reading clinic and was telling prospective buyers that she had taught me how to read using her methodology. I discovered this when a buyer of the franchise called to ask me some questions! Eleanor was often discounted when someone would say, "I wish you had met me first. It wouldn't have taken me 13 months to teach you to read."

A WOMAN FROM Florida heard me speak and afterwards came up to me and said, "Mr. Corcoran, I could teach you not to point as you read. Pointing is a crutch."

What could I say? I had waited over 40 years for the gift of reading and she didn't want me to point! I didn't respond at first, just smiled. She was not to be deterred, however, and continued to press her point. Finally I said, "Would you allow me to help you get rid of your crutch?" She looked puzzled. "Please remove your eyeglasses and read this book."

She laughed and said, "You made your point."

When Pat Lindamood called with still another suggestion, I was curious but suspicious of any quick fix.

"I think I have some information that would interest you," she said, while I signaled Kathy to pick up the extension phone. "I believe I could help you go beyond your present reading level by using an approach you may not have tried yet. Would you be interested in being tested?"

Oh, no, not tests. I had approximately 300 hours of instruction from my tutor, 1,000 hours of independent study over the first 13 months, and continued to study and practice almost daily for the next four years. I was beginning to read phonetically, and now this lady said I didn't have the whole picture. Actually, she was right. I mispronounced words, my sentences dangled in midair, my spelling was abominable (*abonabull*) and many unfamiliar words were still a mystery to unlock.

I had always believed tests were designed to trick me. But after talking to Pat several times on the phone, I realized she was a professional educator with a successful track record.

She came to our home and tested me with little colored blocks and a series of nonsense word patterns. I asked her why she didn't use real words, and she said, "Because I want you to concentrate on the sounds in the patterns of letters and not be distracted by the meanings of words."

It all seemed so foolish at first, but I discovered on my first try that I couldn't even manage a two-sound pattern. It wasn't that I couldn't hear what she was saying, I couldn't distinguish when the sounds changed. That was the underlying problem. It was as simple as that.

She explained some of the multisensory methods they used to help people like me learn to discriminate sound differences. For example, I couldn't process the difference between certain sounds, like *d* and *t*.

I began to get excited. "If this really does what you say," I told Pat, "I need it...and the world needs it."

"Why don't you come and spend some time at our clinic?" she said. "You will know within three or four days if it will be worthwhile to continue with our processing procedures." All my life I had been a risk-taker, and this didn't seem like a big hurdle.

I had been a walking wounded, and Eleanor stopped my bleeding and bound my wounds. Pat performed the surgery that put me on the road to health.

Without hesitation, Kathy and I set out for San Luis Obispo and the Lindamood-Bell clinic for the next "cure." Pat told me she had some medicine, and I wanted it as badly as if I had cancer and was going for a new experimental remedy.

On our way, I thought about what Pat had said about my oral language skills, and how I could miss some important instructions or communications. I knew I had developed some strategies to cope with this lack. They filled my mind as we drove six hours from Oceanside to the Central Coast university town where Cal Poly San Luis Obispo is located.

Neither Kathy nor I knew quite what to expect, but we were both willing to give our all at the clinic. Now I understand that Kathy was afraid she might have to tutor me forever. She didn't know she was about to witness a great breakthrough.

We had canceled vacation plans, rented an apartment without a telephone or television, and didn't tell anyone except our immediate family where we were. The tests began and my scores were very revealing. My word attack (the ability to figure out how to read new words) was at the second-grade level. My spelling was at the fourth-grade level because I had memorized how to spell some words. In addition, my comprehension was incomplete because I would lose the understanding of the big picture as I attempted to decode the next word in front of me. I told Pat that I had to reread some things several times before I could understand them. She said I was trying so hard to sound out words that I couldn't grasp the whole meaning as I read.

Eleanor had taught me the concept of how sounds and letters are linked together, which I understood intellectually. However, I remember listening to a discussion Kathy and Eleanor had as we drove to a speaking engagement. They were sharing their observations about my reading skills and both agreed that I still had a great deal of difficulty connecting certain sounds with corresponding letters.

Eleanor said, "Some sounds he gets quickly; but others we work and work on, and he just doesn't get them."

That is why I was continuing to mispronounce, misspell, and misread so many words.

Pat told me that good readers can automatically match what they see with what they say and hear. I couldn't do that to save my soul. The methodology she was going to introduce to me was more intense phonics and it was getting to the core of my problem. (See Appendix.)

Another problem was identified: I had problems following oral directions and had some problems with reading comprehension. I couldn't easily change what I read into mental pictures. Many times I needed oral directions repeated. In an attempt not to appear dumb, I never asked the same person the same question. Also, if oral instructions were too long or complicated, I would get lost at the beginning. My thoughts started and stopped, like a rabbit changing direction to distract a fox.

Kathy said, "He was a good communicator, but he repeated himself a lot."

I thought people needed to have things repeated!

When I was asked a question, my answer sometimes went so far afield I couldn't tell I had missed the main point until someone said, "That's not what I asked."

Pat wrote in her evaluation of my tests: "These difficulties in reading, spelling, oral and written language expression have made educational instruction very difficult for John in the past."

I could have told her that without taking all those tests! But I liked having it formally validated.

I thought back to how I was famous in school for giving people nicknames because I couldn't read or pronounce their real names. They never knew the reason; they just thought I was a character. If I didn't understand something, I would always talk around it, saying what I thought they said, but adding "unless you mean...." Kathy began to understand why she automatically filled in or completed sentences for me. When she learned that oral language skills are linked to illiteracy, she understood some of the reasons for my language inadequacies.

I began to realize what energy it had taken to be forced to go to plan B if I had been misunderstood. I could *never* be wrong. Being wrong and admitting it might give someone an opening to investigate further and find out my secret.

AS I SAT in the waiting room of the clinic, I observed the stream of hopefuls, all seeking some sort of a miracle for their learning problems. Parents and grandparents brought children, and a few adults came who could spend the time and money. I watched one family with two boys, ages eight and 15. The younger child was Johnny Innocent, the teenager was the Native Alien, with pent-up anger and frustration. I saw myself in both of them; nothing had changed.

I tried not to show it, but Kathy knew I was more apprehensive about this new challenge than I ever was starting a building project. I was back in the second grade again, only now I had a lifetime of experiences, successes, and failures. Would I really be able to get out of the dumb row this time?

My intensive treatment began in August 1991. I plunged into my sessions like a marine about to go into combat. After one week of training four hours daily, I knew something was happening. I asked for my treatment to be increased to six hours a day. I had tested the waters, and I was ready to take the plunge.

The initial focus was on stimulation of phonemic awareness, or auditory conceptual functions, and how this would give me the ability to self-correct my decoding and spelling. I thought that if I went into the operating room, some world-renowned surgeon would be teaching me, but my instructors were college students working in summer jobs.

Steve was one of the clinicians who had overcome a severe reading problem. He was a bright premed student who wanted to be a doctor and knew he would have to conquer his reading problem before he could attend medical school. He had the same passion as I did for learning and sharing with others. We were like patients in a veterans hospital who knew the pain of battle and were recovering.

Those young people had a level of excitement and enthusiasm that is the key to good teaching. They were as thrilled as I was with each step I took. I was impressed with their skills and realized it doesn't take an advanced degree to teach what I had to learn. I learned that to read and spell to my highest potential, I needed to be able to tell how many sounds are in a word, exactly which sounds there are, and the exact order of those sounds.

While Pat Lindamood performed the surgery and prescribed the medicine, the clinicians worked my learning muscles in daily "physical therapy." This new method was teaching me to use my own physical senses in a way I can only describe as *total immersion.*

Using not only my eyes and ears but also mouth movements, I now could understand the phonics Eleanor had worked so hard to teach me.

My clinicians were special people, every one of them. Those young people all had a certain sense of confidence about themselves; they were no-nonsense during the sessions. At times my shirt would be soaking wet as I strained to learn the new techniques. I never worked so hard at anything in my life, and I never felt so good.

For a man who had been used to running the project, I realized that I was not in charge. I couldn't have any pretense with the college students. In order to be teachable, I needed to be vulnerable. I would sit at a table with a young clinician, discovering how my mouth formed sounds and moving little colored blocks in the proper sequence to show the number, sameness or difference, and order of the sounds when they formed words.

When I looked in a mirror to see how my mouth worked to produce an *A*, I saw my mouth in a smile position. *M* was with my lips closed, so the air had to go through my nose. *P* was made by popping my lips. Taking how those sounds felt when I said them and translating them into letters, I began to sort out what makes a word.

With the blocks, we would show separate sounds with different colors. When asked to show the sounds in the nonsense word *hap*, I would pull out blue, red, and white blocks to signify three different sounds. I was learning to distinguish three sounds by my mouth movements. Eventually, I could go on to four sounds, and then five. (Most English words have no more than five sounds in one syllable.) When I could deal with one-syllable words successfully, then I could progress to two-, three-, four-, and five-syllable words.

Kathy came to many sessions with me, especially when new lessons were introduced. The first week of the clinic I gave her permission, for the first time in my life, to correct me. This was a big shift for me! Before, I became angry when Kathy corrected me and I would say, "Oh, you know what I mean." Now I felt she was trying to help me develop some new skills to say what I meant.

Kathy said she had a new appreciation for communication, and she marveled with me how she could learn to use the small colored blocks to help me count the sounds in a word pattern. She could see the value in checking out mouth movements in the mirror and we both began to wonder why this wasn't taught in all the schools as a regular practice.

One little window at a time was opened. I would walk back to our apartment, popping my Ps and humming my Ms like someone who has just discovered a new language. In reality, I had — English. The Native Alien was beginning to get his citizenship papers.

About the third week, all the pieces started falling into place. As Patricia, one of my clinicians, said, "The task went from being hard, physical labor to a fun learning activity."

I felt my own transition from being physically and mentally exhausted to being relaxed and confident. My old enemies, the literates, were becoming my friends. I didn't need to manipulate to protect myself. I could even let go of my Superman image, a subpersonality I had developed long ago to help me overcome my deficits.

In learning to monitor my own speech, I listened to a tape of a talk I had given to a group of educators. I caught the mispronounced Ls, Ts, and Ds in words. I'd never been able to do that before. Through this new "mouth movement" methodology, my brain had awakened.

I had never consciously thought about how my tongue, lips, throat, nose, and the air affected the sounds that came out of my mouth. Feeling and watching myself in a mirror while my tongue and lips formed a sound were what made it click for me. Until then, my hearing and vision processing had failed me with certain sounds; but now, using my kinesthetic sense, I was finally able to get it.

It was like coming out of a coma.

As I discovered how my mouth formed each of the 44 sounds that make up the English language, I was learning those sounds that had troubled me. Helen Keller must have felt like that when she discovered her first word, *water* — that dramatic moment when her teacher, Anne Sullivan, was able to break through to help Helen understand language.

We continued at the clinic through four life-changing weeks, with Pat Lindamood and Nanci Bell (partners in the clinic's work) at the helm, telling the tutors what I needed next. They were able to give me the tools to learn how to think about reading, spelling, and language comprehension.

I was breaking barriers I previously had thought were humanly impossible, like when the seven-foot mark was broken for the high jump. Eleanor had taken me to the tryouts, and the clinic got me over the top.

I once heard about a child who needed glasses but who wasn't properly diagnosed until she was in the sixth grade. When the eye doctor put on her first pair of glasses, she went up to the aquarium in his office and touched the sides. Her face said it all; she couldn't believe the beauty of the fish. Like her, I couldn't believe the beauty of words and how they worked. Before I didn't even know which words were hard or which were easy to spell and read. They were all impossible!

People who have trouble reading and spelling, although they are bright and may do well in math, may be called dyslexic. Dyslexics may add sounds to words, like spelling or reading a word as "stastistics," instead of *statistics*. Or we leave out sounds, like reading the word *stream* as "steam." I thought back to my teaching years and how my young student, Gary, had kidded me for months about saying "libary" for *library*. Through the years I must have used more malapropisms than Mrs. Malaprop herself. (I couldn't judge that I was saying "underlining" when I meant *underlying*.)

It's estimated that one out of three people with normal hearing ability do not have fully developed auditory conceptual ability. Most of their parents and teachers, and the persons themselves, do not realize this. That means that a large percentage of people are missing a skill vital for decoding (*essential* in reading) and spelling.

DURING MY FIRST few days at the clinic, I met Josh. We were standing in line for the men's room when he gave me a little push and said, "Can I go in front of you?" I looked at him and knew his antsy behavior had more to do with his impulsiveness than a full bladder and said, "No, wait your turn."

He stepped back and said, "Oh, bummer."

He was only ten years old, but we had so much in common that we soon became fast friends. He had just finished fourth grade and couldn't read, comprehend complex language, follow directions, or express himself clearly. He was also very withdrawn because he thought he was dumb. How well I remembered Johnny, the kid who was labeled Buzzard in his reading class. My heart went out to Josh. Here was a boy from an accomplished, literate family. His father was a mid-level officer in the State Department in the Bush and Clinton administrations, his mother a skilled nurse. Their home was filled with books and stimulating conversation. But Josh, who had been passed from grade to grade without being able to master simple reading exercises, had retreated into his own world of inadequacy. His teachers said, "Boys tend to be slow learners; don't worry about him."

One night Josh's parents, Larry and Sue, invited us to dinner at a Chinese restaurant. After we ordered, I turned to Josh and said, "Do you have any brothers or sisters?"

Small talk is not easy for illiterates. Josh did not mean to be rude, but he answered, "If I had any brothers or sisters, wouldn't they be here?"

His parents were embarrassed, but I understood. At times I don't like to waste words and frequently interrupt people, but much of what others may see as inappropriate social behavior is not rooted in disrespect. It has more to do with our inadequacies in oral expression. Although I do believe parents must teach these children how to behave in social situations, they also must have an understanding of their child.

Another time, Kathy and I went to church with Pat. There was a time for prayer requests, and Pat asked for special prayers to help Josh learn because he was a real challenge for her. What we didn't know was that Josh was in church too, and he blurted out with a very loud voice, "Yeah, and I want to get out of special ed."

Josh spent a month at the clinic, working four hours a day with his instructors, learning to identify and track sounds and make mental pictures for comprehension. We've stayed in touch with each other and I see him frequently when I go to Washington, D.C. Best of all, when he entered fifth grade, he could read at a level with his classmates.

AS I BEGAN to hear and understand sounds and apply them to letters and words, I discovered a whole new world. In some ways it was like returning to first grade and skipping to the next grade every week. I wanted to say "aha!" when what I said matched what I saw. *Now I get it!* For the first time in many years I remembered my special song — "Zip-a-dee-doo-dah" — that had given me so much courage as a child. All of a sudden there was plenty of sunshine coming my way. Now the words weren't just a cover to hide my fears. I was truly beginning to understand. The days were getting better.

Although I had taught school and had given instructions to contractors, secretaries, lawyers, and coworkers in my construction and development business, I always knew my oral skills were inadequate; another missing piece.

To improve my oral language, I needed to be able to correctly express myself without allowing my thoughts to float into limbo or shoot off like an endless rocket. The process of learning to read had trained my mind to be more focused and more able to concentrate, which improved my oral expression. It's not enough to be able to read or listen to words; we must also get meaning from what we see and hear. This is a process Nanci Bell calls Visualizing and Verbalizing. (See Appendix.)

AFTER ONE MONTH of instruction in the Lindamood-Bell Learning Processes, with 100 hours of treatment — four-fifths of the time on auditory conceptual development and one-fifth on concept imagery or visualizing and verbalizing — I gained ten years in word-attack skill (from second-grade to the 12th-grade level); three years in word recognition (from fifth- to eighth-grade level); and a year and a half in spelling. The gain in spelling was stronger than my score indicated because now I had more phonetic than unphonetic errors. For instance, whereas I previously spelled material, "mattial," now I spelled it matirial; precious, "prest," now presious; physician, "phyustion," now "physistion." Ability to spell phonetically is the first step toward overall improvement in spelling.

In addition, the stimulation of concept imagery enabled me to improve from the 25th to the 84th percentile in following oral directions, and from the 60th to the 87th percentile in reading comprehension. (Normal would range approximately from the 40th to the 60th percentile, and low normal would range approximately from the 20th to the 40th percentile.)

AT THE END of my month of training, Kathy says today, she started to notice a personality change. "John wasn't as defensive — and he did something he had never done before in our 27 years of marriage. He apologized directly to me and meant it.

"He always teased me as a way out of a direct apology. When he was at fault, and he knew it, he would say, 'Now, Kathy, don't you think you should say you're sorry for that?' I know that was his way of apologizing, but it always bothered me."

It surprised me to see tears in Kathy's eyes when I said to her, "Kathy, I'm really sorry." I knew something good was happening because I had begun to feel better about myself. That self-image, bruised since childhood, was healing.

However, the old anger still simmered. It's like the person who has been a hostage in an enemy country who, when released, goes home to a parade and celebrations. When the exhilaration wears off, the questions begin to nag: *Why me? Why was I a hostage? Why was I treated so badly? Why wasn't I released sooner?*

When I saw how those programs worked, I was angry at what I had missed. Larry Johnson, the father of my young friend, Josh, said, "This method should be available to the public at large. Every student and every teacher should be tested for phonological skills. The reading levels of millions could be changed." Larry added that he learned more about the English language in four weeks of accompanying Josh to the clinic than he did working on his Ph.D.

My excitement was high as my learning skills improved. I read words that I had skipped before: Sounds blended with letters, and I began to understand that a sentence could have an ending.

A few months later, I was traveling on a plane and came across a word I didn't recognize. At first, I just skipped over it, but then I said to myself, *No, you can decode it.* I worked at phonetically breaking it down and when I was successful, I looked at the word *inconspicuous* and said out loud, "Oh, *that's* what you look like!" (Several heads turned.) It was a 25-cent word I had used many times, but then, all of a sudden, it was like seeing for the first time a person I had done business with over the phone for 20 years.

Of course, these things didn't happen overnight. And I was only beginning my journey on the road to reading, writing, and spelling.

People who have trouble learning can become successful in reading and spelling when the root of the problem is diagnosed. For the millions of children entering private or public schools, early diagnosis can prevent many future literacy problems.

My experience fueled my desire to do something to help others who struggled as I had. This was the beginning of a dream that began to develop into reality. (See Appendix)

PHONICS ADVOCATES ASSUME that all people can identify and classify speech sounds, judge relationships between sounds, and track sounds in sequence. There is evidence that 25 to 30 percent of the population cannot do this easily. I know those skills didn't come naturally to me. Many teachers will say that phonics doesn't work for everyone. Phonics does work, if the proper foundation is established. (That's the builder in me talking!)

Combining phonics with the auditory discrimination in depth (LIPS) program is what I will call the *Complete Intensive Systematic Phonics Learning System*. If anyone has a simpler title, I'm certainly open to it.

FIRST: *Testing the "soil" for reading involves determining that a student has the ability to identify and classify speech sounds, to judge the relationship between sounds, and to identify sounds in sequence.*

In most places in California, a soils test is mandated before you can get a permit to build. We want to make sure that a home is not built on poor or expansive ground. I have seen homes that were built before this test was law, and many have slid off their faulty foundations. The same is certainly true for building literacy.

SECOND: *The best foundation is phonics, if "soils testing" reveals there is solid ground upon which to build.*

If you decided to build a house, the layout and design would be the equivalent of emotional aesthetics, but the most important element is the foundation. Today we use concrete and steel. A good builder, like a good teacher, uses the best tools and material available, which includes a plan and blueprints.

Some phonics advocates acknowledge that a small percentage of the population can't learn to read with a conventional phonics program alone; but I believe the number is much higher than their estimates. There are many of us who need the "soils test" before starting to build on the foundational phonics.

Today we have research-based predictive assessment tests that could be given to kindergartners, first-, and second-graders to diagnose a child's level of phonemic awareness. If we can set standards to build a house, why not set mandatory standards for testing children's phonemic awareness before teaching begins?

There's no denying it — it's hard work for some of us to learn to read. We need teachers and students motivated to achieve results. But judging from my own experience, I believe almost anyone can learn to read, write, and spell. Proper instruction is clearly the key!

As Jonathan Kozol asked in *Illiterate America*, "What can be done to guarantee that children now in school, or those about to enter school, will not become another generation of adult nonreaders in another ten or twenty years?"[1]

When will we give the time and attention needed at the beginning stage of reading to prevent illiteracy? We have the tools for prevention now.

America's educational system is cracked; the schoolhouse is slipping off its faulty foundation. We cannot afford to take shortcuts. Let's not skip the need to test for and develop the solid ground of phonemic awareness under the foundation of phonics.

I felt that God had given me a gift, and that I must share it. I had made many speeches about learning to read at the age of 48, but that was just a start. Four years later, a whole new world had opened.

Two summers after my first experience at the clinic, that point really came home to me. I was speaking at a conference in Philadelphia when a young woman came up to me afterward, sobbing with tears of rage. She had reached a certain level in her literacy improvement but felt stymied, just as I had. She wanted the missing element spread to others who couldn't afford my clinical experience. She said, "You got the medicine that is too expensive for me and others like me."

I'll never forget her. It was then I asked God to help me make this available to the masses, to help not just special people or the privileged who could afford it, but to give everyone the opportunity to walk confidently, freely, into the world of spoken and written language.

WHEN I FIRST entered the literacy center, struggling with putting my thoughts into words, I remember saying I wanted to write a book. How ridiculous that was then. Now I have realized some of my dreams and goals. But the next step is to help some of the 93 million Americans, like the woman from Philadelphia, to reach some of their goals. As a result, the John Corcoran Foundation, Inc., has been established:

OUR MISSION

The mission of the John Corcoran Foundation, Inc., is to facilitate the prevention and eradication of illiteracy in adults and children across America, through public aware-ness, creation and dissemination of resources, training and mentoring through existing literacy organizations and edu-cational programs.

OUR VISION

Our vision is to help create a society in which each indi-vidual has the basic skills necessary to become a success in all aspects of life including education, work and community service.

We never know how small decisions and chance encounters can change our lives.

CHAPTER 16

The Healing of America

To come from being an illiterate with so-called learning disabilities to knowing how to read and write was like being rescued after 72 days afloat at sea. I wish I had been rescued sooner, but at the time I was too overcome with joy to dwell on it.

But what about all the others — the 93 million adults in America who lack the literacy skills they need to survive, let alone compete, in today's technologically advanced society? These are the individuals who make up what I call the "subculture of illiteracy." They are the misunderstood, the angry, the manipulators, the outcasts. For their sake — and for all our sakes — they, too, must be shown the way out.

I remember the case several years ago of a California mother who contended that her ten-year-old son made it to the fifth grade without being able to read, so she filed a lawsuit seeking to close down the boy's school. The mother's lawyer said, "I have no idea how they kept passing him at each grade level." The superintendent of schools insisted that it was highly unlikely that a student in his district could fail to make progress in reading for so long without a teacher noticing and taking action. But that kind of neglect is happening every day in our schools.

So what happens when a child who cannot read or write becomes an adult who lacks literacy skills? What becomes of those who are pushed through or drop out without getting what every child is entitled to receive in America's public schools: the compulsory education that includes the imparting of knowledge of how to read, write, and spell? Consider the words of the parole officer who told me, "Most of my parolees have mainstreamed their way through school." This means they slid through without learning the basics in reading, writing, spelling, or math, but they graduated with a diploma. They are not the only ones.

Joyce, a woman with an infectious smile and a lively sense of humor, recalled how her mother had wanted her to attend a certain prep school. During the interview, the headmaster asked her what kinds of books she liked to read. "I didn't know what to say because I didn't know how to read. I remembered that in fourth grade a teacher read a Nancy Drew mystery to us, so I said, 'Nancy Drew mysteries.' My mother was indignant. She said, 'You read that trash?' I wanted to tell her the truth but I just couldn't."

Joyce didn't get into the prep school, but she did go to a local high school — and graduated. She *still* couldn't read.

Malcolm spoke painfully about his dyslexia, which he discovered he had about eight years earlier. "When I was 16 years old," he recalled, "I couldn't say my name in public. I was raised in a family of engineers, but I couldn't add. I went to a prestigious college because I was an athlete — a very angry athlete. However, I learned to memorize in order to pass tests."

Then one day Malcolm began to consider what to do with his life. That's when he discovered the world of art. "I didn't have words to express myself, so art became my language. My hero was (French sculptor Auguste) Rodin, because I heard that he had been sent home with a note that said, 'We cannot educate this man.' The master sculptor who gave us *The Thinker* and many other masterpieces was dyslexic."

Bob told me, "The biggest problem in dealing with dyslexia is the nonrecognition in the school system."

An emerging literate as I was at the time we spoke, Bob recalled how misinformed teachers were, how they viewed a student's inability to read as misbehavior or a case of not trying hard enough. "When I was in second grade for the second year, the teacher said, 'If you don't learn to read this book, I'll keep you in here for another year.' Whoa! I didn't want to do that, so I got the old Dick and Jane reader, had my stepfather read it to me, and I memorized it."

Bob continued with his saga. "In fourth grade the teacher said, 'Bobby, you write like someone with Old English script. I can't read any of it.' I couldn't decipher any of my writing, either. In high school, my algebra teacher said to me after I had been in his class for three years, 'I'm going to pass you because I can't teach you anything!'"

Looking back, Bob wondered where the help was for him when he needed it; why didn't teachers recognize that he needed special instruction in order to learn how to read? "People are being destroyed with the callous attitude of those who can't or won't teach them the basics."

The words these adults speak echo the hurts they endured as children. They felt left out, shunned, ignored. They are so used to hiding their lack of literacy skills that they have made themselves invisible. Even as they acquire the skills as adults, they remain in touch with those wounded children and teenagers they once were, who spent years in school and watched as others learned how to read, write, and spell, while they went away empty.

My diagnosis was a severe auditory discrimination problem. My inability to distinguish the difference between the sounds made by letter and groups of letters made it impossible for me to learn how to read — until I was an adult and I received the proper instruction necessary to help me "crack the code." All that time, however, my real disability was not dyslexia or another learning deficiency. Illiteracy was my real disability.

Since I began speaking at conferences and attending workshops, I have heard so many different definitions of learning disabilities and dyslexia that it's no wonder people are confused. Many people think it means seeing letters backwards, even though there is no evidence to support this view. The experts have many definitions for dyslexia, but in essence it is a reading and/or language dysfunction. The International Dyslexia Association (IDA) states:

> "Dyslexia refers to a cluster of symptoms, which result in people having difficulties with specific language skills, particularly reading. Students with dyslexia usually experience difficulties with other language skills such as spelling, writing, and pronouncing words. Dyslexia affects individuals throughout their lives; however, its impact can change at different stages in a person's life. It is referred to as a learning disability because dyslexia can make it very difficult for a student to succeed academically in the typical instructional environment, and in its more severe forms, will qualify a student for special education, special accommodations, or extra support services."

Dyslexia is caused by neurobiological and genetic factors, according to IDA. It added that 15 to 20 percent of the population has a language-based learning disability. Of the students with specific learning disabilities who receive special education services, 70 to 80 percent have deficits in reading. "Dyslexia is the most common cause of reading, writing, and spelling difficulties."[1]

Perhaps no one truly appreciates the value of reading as much as those who cannot read. Those who dwell in the subculture of illiteracy, outsiders among the dominate culture of the written word, understand its power because they do not have it. They are the ones for whom a street sign, a menu, instructions to operate an appliance, a job application, a newspaper article, or an email is as daunting as the most impossible task.

A few decades ago, someone who had only the most basic of literacy skills could probably find a job. In today's technologically advanced society, mastery of the written word is prerequisite for opportunity.

With so many adults lacking adequate literacy skills, where is there hope? It is there because I am walking proof that people who have difficulty with the written word can master it. I also believe I am representative of adult learners, including the hundreds whom I have met over the years. (I beg to differ with the newspaper reporter who once said I was atypical.) I was as typical as millions of other people who have difficulty reading. There are many more success stories, yet there are millions of people who are still hiding, not believing they can really find help or be helped.

My motivation to learn how to read came out of desperation. Fortunately, at the same time, the country was becoming aware of the desperation of millions of other people like me. However, motivating nonreaders is only half of the picture. New readers need to find emotional support and healing. We are like prisoners of war; we carry our scars.

Many of us also need to become missionaries. In order to become strong literacy advocates, we must be informed. That's why I became like an investigative reporter, talking to other emerging literates and reading — yes, *reading* — literacy-related books and journals, and adding to my "library of people."

One of those people was Dr. Ann Schafer, whom I met at a conference. She had experience in research and in teaching students with learning disabilities. New doors to my mind and emotions were opened at that time. I told her that, in the years when I couldn't read or write, I felt like I was hiding underground to escape the literates who were my enemies. As I told her about the tactics I had used to escape detection, she nodded. "That's normal for someone in your situation, John," she said.

What a relief to know that I was "normal."

She told me about the behavior patterns many learning disabled/ dyslexics use to cope. We wear many masks: The obsessive/compulsive person may act rigidly to control his world; the impulsive person may act outrageously and get undue attention; the indifferent person may be a loner and aloof; the risk-taker may cover his mistakes with reckless abandonment; the bored person may act disinterested about learning; the angry person often acts with an I'd-rather-be-bad-than-stupid attitude; the clown prefers to draw attention away from his shortcomings to gain approval....

She seemed to be describing me!

Dr. Schafer shared her personal experiences of helping parents handle the grief of having borne "the disappointing child." Parents would sometimes blame each other, but they always want to know "why?" She was convinced, as I am, that if we could only teach every child *all* the ways to learn to decode — a kind of total-immersion phonetic approach like I benefited from — we could eradicate illiteracy at the preventive level.

"Children are sponges," she reminded me. "They think, *I want to please my teacher*: Children want to love and be loved, but when they think they are dumb, they develop one of those subpersonalities as a defense. Someone needs to look into the eyes of a child and say, 'You're God's best. You're special.' What parents hear from the teachers is: 'Johnny isn't paying attention; he's distracting the other children,' or 'Sally is not studying hard enough.'"

With that negative attitude, Johnny and Sally may never learn how to read or write, and even if they do it may be at a minimal level. This kind of child abuse brings about the subpersonalities, which do not always serve them well as adults.

Dr. Schafer has been a champion who never gives up hope. Her belief is so strong, it is like telling people who cannot walk that they will defy the odds and become marathon runners. "Until I find someone I absolutely cannot teach to read, I will continue to try," Dr. Schafer said.

She has taught many seemingly hopeless cases that others unsuccessfully tried to teach. With her intensive, systematic phonics and auditory processing methodology, she has been successful.

We know what works in teaching children how to read. The National Reading Panel has conducted research on reading instruction and has identified five key elements:

- Phonemic awareness
- Phonics
- Fluency
- Vocabulary
- Text Comprehension

The National Reading Panel found that "effective reading instruction includes teaching children to break apart and manipulate the sounds in words (phonemic awareness), teaching them these sounds are represented by letters of the alphabet which can then be blended together to form words (phonics), having them practice what they've learned by reading aloud with guidance and feedback (guided oral reading), and applying reading comprehension strategies to guide and improve reading comprehension."

The panel also stressed the importance of systematic phonics instruction for children with learning disabilities. "…(B)ecause children vary in reading ability and vary in the skills they bring to the classroom, no single approach to teaching phonics could be used in all cases. For this reason, it is important to train teachers in the different kinds of approaches to teaching phonics and in how to tailor these approaches to particular groups of students."[2]

The research tells us what works to teach all learners — including those with learning difficulties — how to read. Now it's our job to implement it, to make sure our teachers are properly trained in the knowledge and methodologies that can address the needs of all learners, both adults and children. No matter the age, every learner deserves a chance to attain the same literacy skills as everyone else. Having access to the written word is the key to education, and education is the great equalizer in this country. Without literacy, a person is condemned to being a second-class citizen.

Learning how to read as an adult is a powerful experience. Although it is a positive transformation, it uncovers deep-seated feelings that must also be addressed. How we act and how we feel are not always the same. Emerging literates seem to pass through stages of grief, just as those who have experienced major losses in their lives. There seemed to be a similar process I went through as I became literate.

Those steps included: *Denial.* I wanted to hide that I was illiterate, even though passing as a literate took all of the energy I had. *Anger.* Beneath the façade was the resentment toward those who didn't or couldn't teach me as a child. *Bargaining.* I pleaded with God; I promised Him unrealistic exchanges if He would perform a sudden, lightning-bolt miracle. *Depression.* My depression came out of a feeling of hopelessness. *Acceptance.* Once I learned to read, I could ask for forgiveness for my sins of deception. Finally, I could forgive my teachers, the educational system, my parents, and myself.

Many people — such as veterans, battered spouses, or victims of sexual abuse — suffer post-traumatic stress syndrome or flashbacks to unpleasant experiences. Anytime the brain is reminded of those past experiences, emotions are triggered. (Ask me about grown men who cry when giving a speech before an audience.) A healing experience is needed to resolve this pain. As I began to experience healing, my anger and hurt were gradually replaced by the desire to help others break out of illiteracy bondage and experience their own healing.

America heals as her people heal. Although I have great respect for professionals who have studied the problem of illiteracy and are attempting to find and implement solutions, I do not believe that the government or our entrenched school system has all the necessary medicine for our wounded. Churches and community groups must become more involved in providing aid for this epidemic. The business community also needs to realize that it plays an important part in providing solutions.

This is the challenge: an Olympics-sized race that can only be won by relay runners. Everyone needs to grab the baton and pass it on. We are not competing against one another. We are all on the same team. Here are some of the milestones I suggest. After all, I have been training for this competition all my life.

1. *Teach intensive, systematic phonics to everyone, and insist that all teachers be properly trained to accomplish this.* This should include multisensory methods such as the ones I experienced in the auditory discrimination program.

Teachers must be given proper training. Some of them have severe phonemic awareness problems themselves and are unable to teach phonics properly. This corrective help was not available to them during their academic training, but it can be given now. Otherwise they will feel inadequate, ineffective, and unprepared. If they are to effectively teach beginning readers, they will need special training. It can be done.

As a new adult reader, I know that phonics was the cornerstone for my developing literacy. As a graduate of a public library literacy program where I was phonetically taught, I am a strong supporter of volunteer literacy providers for adults. Learning how to read is like learning how to play the piano. It requires skilled teachers and practice, practice, and more practice.

After I graduated from my volunteer program, I worked independently for almost four years. However, I felt like a marathon runner who hits the invisible brick wall a mile from the finish line. I just couldn't break through the barrier. I needed a coach, a professional who could diagnose my weakness and prescribe a treatment. I sought and found that help. There is a saying: "When the student is ready, the teacher appears." That was certainly my experience with Pat Lindamood.

For adults like me who need that extra help, I expect volunteer groups to get advanced training, and I expect community college and universities to commit to educating adult illiterates and to properly train teachers. For this battle to be won, it will require professional soldiers, as well as a volunteer army.

2. *Require reading and writing to be taught at every level from pre-school to the university level.* I would go so far as to recommend a Hippocratic-type oath for teachers, a solemn pledge to teach all students to read. A teacher must believe that every child's brain has the potential for literacy unless there is medical evidence that an individual child is incapable of learning to read.

3. *Eliminate labeling.* We are survivors of what I consider a misuse of language. This is not about political correctness, but human dignity. Therefore, I think the term "learning disabled" should be discarded. I was *able* to learn many things; I just had difficulty learning to read. I prefer the term learning *difficulties.*

I also dislike the term "slow learner." I was fast when it came to numbers, but I needed more time with reading. For some of us, there are no shortcuts. Most so-called slow learners are not slow intellectually, and many are often street-smart kids. However, they may be hands-on learners who do not understand the material until they have thoroughly experienced it.

We humans tend to live up (or down) to the descriptions given to us. Labels can damage. There is also the danger of a self-fulfilling prophecy by accepting a label. We reap what we sow, and that includes negativity. The only reason people didn't treat me like an illiterate was because I didn't tell them my secret.

4. *Overhaul special education classes.* Special education needs to be more than a holding tank. I know there is very good intent in

many special education programs, but it has not produced quality results. I do not want to imply that we do not need well-trained special education teachers. But by their own admission the majority of them have had little or no remedial reading training. We need a more targeted approach to meet the learning needs of students in special education — the majority of whom are there only because they have a reading deficiency. With systematic, direct instruction, these students could be brought to grade level in reading and — as I have seen in many individual circumstances — brought out of the special education program and into the mainstream.

5. *Focus on family literacy programs and community outreach.* We have inherited generations of uneducated parents who simply cannot teach their children to read because they are illiterate. The literate society must intervene to break this cycle of failure.

I believe family literacy programs can do a great service by teaching parents and preparing children for learning. The National Center for Family Literacy has done an outstanding job of spearheading the development of community programs that help families learn. Another champion is the Barbara Bush Foundation for Family Literacy.

The late Senator Paul Simon, who had been a leader in Congress on literacy issues, once said, "The great division of our society is not between black and white, Hispanic and Anglo, and all other divisions; the great division is between people who have hope and people who have given up. Family literacy gives people that spark of hope and will continue to provide it if we adopt the right policies."[3]

6. *Encourage grassroots involvement.* People with a passion for justice make a difference. They don't need public assistance or government funds.

Some of the leaders in the literacy movement are in San Diego. Volunteer adult education and community college programs, public library programs, and other community-based organizations have formed the San Diego Council on Literacy. Jose Cruz, who is now CEO of the San Diego Council on Literacy, was once the enthusiastic literacy services coordinator at the Council. He observed: "This is a grassroots movement that has drawn community leaders and literacy service providers together in a voluntary coalition." Among other services, the Council provides tutor training materials upon request and has sent copies throughout the U.S. and Canada.

The *San Diego Union Tribune*, under the ownership of the late Helen Copley, took up the cause of literacy as a crusade, including with fundraisers for the Council on Literacy. These public-service efforts also contributed to community awareness.

One of the challenges in the San Diego area is providing quality education *in English* to the Hispanic community as well as to children whose families have emigrated to the U.S. from other countries. Some people have been led to believe that bilingual education programs and classes were the way to address literacy for Spanish-speaking children and adults.

I am very aware of the controversial and often emotional debate about bilingual education. Those who oppose it are often accused of racial or ethnic bigotry. The number of ESL (English as a Second Language) students (children and adults) are creating a challenge to our commitment and efforts to prevent and eradicate adult illiteracy. And there are some who would like to blame our immigration problems without taking into account our long history (60+ years) of having failed to teach so many of our children how to read. The immigration issue is just another distraction that delays us in solving our long standing illiteracy problem. We need to focus on proper instruction and properly trained teachers. I have walked the walk as the Native Alien, and I earnestly want my illiterate Hispanic brothers and sisters to learn how to read, write, and improve their oral language skills as I have. My motive is clear.

In Texas, a group called Hispanics for English Language Proficiency (HELP) conducted a survey several years ago among Latino parents, and the results were overwhelmingly in favor of having their children learn basic skills in English. More than 10 years ago, in Oceanside, California, schools officials phased out bilingual education in favor of providing instruction in English with teachers who are specially trained in English as a second language. The acceptance of the approach by Hispanic parents has been very high.

At the grassroots levels, churches and other community organizations can play another part. Many churches have begun to see the importance of literacy classes. As one church leader said, "We're tired of handing out food that is consumed once. We want to make a difference in people's lives."

I am optimistic. My hope is on the future. I believe America is on its way to being healed of the illiteracy epidemic. It is everybody's business to see that he or she is part of the cure.

When this book was first published in 1994, I was cheered by "Goal Five," which was signed by President George H. W. Bush and the nation's 50 governors at a historic education summit, and later personally endorsed and signed by President Clinton. Goal Five set a target that by the year 2000 every adult American would be literate and would possess the necessary knowledge and skills to compete in a global economy and to exercise the rights and responsibilities of citizenship.

The year 2000 has come and gone, and we are still facing a crisis of illiteracy in America. So how can I remain so hopeful? Because I must, just as I did when I took the first step as an adult learner. In time, I learned to read. What I have done, others can do — and we must do everything we can to help them.

BELOW IS THE second poem I wrote after learning how to write. It is dedicated to all who have given to me and others the gift of literacy.

THE YEAR 2000 HAS COME AND GONE
by John Corcoran

January 2008

Reading words is quite a gain,
And I am not about to complain.
But, I am obligated to explain
Some of our pain, without casting any blame.
We all, we all have something to gain.

Childhood memories ring clear in our ear
And images of failures are still very near.
Oh, how we still fear
That abandonment is near.
Why we still fear is because of what we still hear.

Label, label, learning disable.
Let's put all the cards on the table.
Excuse, an abuse, an excuse not to produce
Just label them disabled.

Perhaps those that can read
Just cannot concede, that our unmet need to read
Is causing this great nation to bleed.
Don't watch us bleed, please teach us to read.

We have a right to grieve
But we must learn now to read.
Don't leave us now, please
Teach us all to read.

The stage is set for basic skills.
Don't expect instant thrills,
It's going to take drills and drills,
Before we have those basics skills.

The year 2000, was our goal
We didn't reach it but we are not too old
To reach a new goal, we must be bold.
And if you agree, back your words with this deed
Roll up your sleeves and teach us to read.

The Journey of a Lifelong Learner

NONE OF US have the ability to turn back time. Our lives play out the way they do. We make decisions and take actions, for better or worse. We learn, we grow; we double back, we leap ahead. We regret and we reminiscence.

Still, we can't help but wonder what we'd change if we could. For me, if I could turn back the hands of time, I'd go back to when I was in the second grade. I'd sit down beside Johnny the Innocent who was in the "dumb row," and I'd make sure I brought along someone on my time travel who could give that child what he needed: research-based, direct, systematic instruction to learn how to read, write, and spell.

Learning to read as a young child would have dramatically changed the course of my life. I wouldn't have spent more than four decades in the subculture of illiteracy. I wouldn't have been the Native Alien, who lashed out, or the college-aged "desperado" who did anything to get by. And I wouldn't have been "the teacher who couldn't read."

There would be no book in your hands right now. So would I trade these pages to rescue one little boy — little Johnny Corcoran, the Innocent — from illiteracy? You bet I would! I truly mean what I say when I state that not teaching a child to read is a form of child neglect and child abuse. So how could I not prevent that from happening, if I could?

Of course, I can't go back and rescue Johnny the Innocent from the dumb row. Where I did have a say in what happened to me, however, was some 20 years ago when I was asked whether I would go public with my story—airing my dirty laundry for all the world to see. I had reservations about doing that, and choosing to do so did cause some conflicts for me over the years. The experience has not always been enjoyable. Having the opportunity to explore my personal experience of illiteracy, however, has afforded me invaluable self-exploration. I have invested 20 years in that process, with all the emotions that go with it, from anger to sorrow, from hope to joy.

On a personal level, I was motivated to delve into my years in the subculture of illiteracy in order to better understand myself. My self-reflection is sometimes prompted by the questions that people ask. Whether they are gentle, probing questions that are attempts to understand, or more sharply worded ones that don't mask the criticism, they are still helpful to my process. In answering them, I go deeper within myself to revisit what I experienced.

When I tell people I thought I was "dumb" when I was a child, some have said, "How could you think you were dumb? You must have been a very intelligent child to survive and thrive as well as you did." While it's a nice compliment, I suppose, I don't want to dwell on how smart Johnny the Innocent was. It was grueling and demoralizing to attend school as a child with the hopes of learning to read. I could not read at any level anywhere near my peers until I was more than sixty years old. Persistence, tenacity, and a yearning pursuit of the American dream of prosperity drove me to continue to go to school and to attend college.

When I was in elementary school, it wasn't long before I became defiant. I never really accepted being put in the dumb row in second grade. I never accepted my own illiteracy even though, as a child, I knew I could not read or write, and I never accepted my own illiteracy as an adult. And today I do not accept the deplorable condition of America's epidemic of illiteracy. It is unacceptable to me that millions of people today are enduring the same unnecessary pain that I experienced for so much of my life.

People who are persistent refuse to allow circumstances to get in their way — regardless of intelligence, knowledge, education, or experience. They simply don't quit. That leads to another question I'm asked, which is usually phrased like this: "So how did you do it?" Without being argumentative, I'm sometimes tempted to answer the question with a question: "Do what?" There is no simple or short answer to their question. Like everyone else's, my life is a complex mosaic of circumstances, opportunities, choices, actions, and consequences. What was consistent throughout, once again, was my stubborn refusal to accept that my inability to read or write was going to limit me.

All that having been said the fact remains that my life mosaic does contains some very large pieces representing those years when I was illiterate. They may not be the prettiest tiles, but they are certainly central to the picture. If I look at it philosophically, I see that since this was my lot in life, I had a responsibility to do something with it. Part of that has been this autobiography, and also writing a second book, *Bridge to Literacy*, in which I explore in greater depth and with dozens of interviews with leading experts, the epidemic of illiteracy and what can be done to address it. That call to action is one of my proudest accomplishments.

Through this journey of relating my personal experiences and, in the process, telling the story of illiteracy in America, I have undergone a tremendous healing. Much of the pain, anger, and guilt I felt have been replaced with triumph and hope — not only for my life, but also for others.

When I began sharing my story publicly 20 years ago, I was motivated to help others. Now that I am a part of literate society, I have the obligation to bridge the misunderstandings about my fellow illiterates. I need to advise others, especially teachers and administrators, not to be fooled by the masks, façades, and defense mechanisms used by those who cannot read. They may appear not to care, to shrug it all off as "no big deal." Don't believe it for a second. *Not being able to read is the "biggest deal" in the life of anyone who is confronted and intimidated by the written word on a daily basis.* It is like starving to death in front of a banquet table, but for some reason you can't get to the food.

When I learned to read I wanted to explain to the literate world the frustrations and survival tactics of the illiterate subculture; but more importantly I wanted everyone to know there is hope and help for others like me. I wanted to move them to compassion, so that they could recognize and seize upon their obligation to help. That was my mission.

In years that I have traveled across the U.S. and Canada and to Europe as a speaker, lecturer, and literacy advocate, I embraced my mission. What grew out of my unwillingness to accept my own illiteracy expanded to championing the rights of all children and adults to learn how to read, write, and spell. When I didn't have all the facts, I did the research. I engaged in discussions with educated people and literate society. I addressed large audiences and had intense one-on-one discussions with all kinds of people. I've talked with teachers, administrators, parents, students, policymakers, inmates, business men and women, and community leaders of every type imaginable. Every interaction was enriching and enlightening for me, even when we didn't agree.

When the stakes are high, the emotions are intense. There are places in this book where I expressed my anger — not with the intent to blame any individual, but simply to reflect the hurt, frustration, and despair that comes from not being able to read. To me, there is no greater threat to the economic and social welfare of this country and the world than illiteracy. It widens the gaps between haves and have-nots and impedes the ability of people, especially of different languages and cultures, to understand each other. Literacy promotes equality, opportunity, and responsibility; it leads to healthier, more cohesive families. Literacy isn't a magic pill for all society's ills, but illiteracy is a caustic acid that eats away at everything. That's why we must persist on this journey, no matter how long or difficult. We cannot give up — ever.

For me, my journey led from being an adult learner to an advocate and a literacy provider. What started as a few speaking engagements grew as more people became interested in literacy and wanted to hear my story. When it became apparent that this was going to take up more and more of my time, I had to create a structure to organize it; to make sure what I was doing and why. The creation of the John Corcoran Foundation was a natural outgrowth of my purpose discovered in the second half of my life.

When it was formed, I gathered a group of supporters who offered to assist me and came up with the Foundation's mission statement. As it states today:

"The mission of the John Corcoran Foundation, Inc., is to facilitate the prevention and eradication of illiteracy in adults and children across America, through public awareness, creation and dissemination of resources, and training and mentoring through existing literacy organizations and educational programs."

With my speaking engagements and appearances related to the first publication of this book, I knew I was accomplishing the awareness piece. In the beginning, however, I wanted to leave the solution part to others. But I found it wasn't enough to address an audience and explain what *they* had to do. I had to walk that talk. The need for the Foundation's two-pronged approach of awareness and providing resources was apparent every time I spoke. Inevitably I would be approached by people wanting to help and also needing help. The Foundation has been my way to respond and to model what others can do in their own communities.

Having had the experience of benefiting from the best instruction available, thanks to my dear friend and mentor, the late Pat Lindamood, I knew I had to make that opportunity available to others. The question was how. As my travels continued, some key players crossed my path. Among them was a teacher in Colorado, Marianne Arling, who today is the programs director for the Foundation and oversees tutoring programs for students in that state.

When I first met Marianne, I was struck by her passion, her vision, and also her persistence. With a master's degree in special education, Marianne had wanted to help struggling students, but she didn't feel that she could do what she needed to in the traditional school environment. After pursuing some training in Lindamood-Bell, Phono-Graphix, and other reading methodologies, Marianne worked with school districts and also a community college, where she trained tutors. When she hooked up with the Foundation, I knew we had found our partner — the one who could help us move into providing solutions.

Today, through the Foundation, Marianne directs after-school reading programs in Colorado that provide tutoring for students who need direct, systematic phonetic instruction and remediation. She is also helping the Foundation to expand the use of technology in literacy, including through a program offered to a virtual charter school whose students are mostly home schooled. In addition the Foundation provides other online literacy programs in California and Colorado.

I believe we are just scratching the surface of what technology can do in literacy. In addition to online tutoring, technology will help us expand our use of diagnostics, assessment, and instruction. While students still need to work with a trained teacher — and often one on one — technology can document the learners' progress and provide the repetition of drills with positive reinforcement, to reach learners wherever and whenever they are available. At the same time, we are putting a powerful tool into the hands of emerging literates. The joyful accomplishment of students who can now use a computer — including typing on a keyboard and searching on the internet — is unimaginable. A part of the world that virtually everyone else accesses without a second thought is suddenly open to them.

Having seen the evolution of my own journey, I can only imagine what the next 20 years will bring. Today, my story is that of a 70-year-old man, but I know I have many fellow travelers out there of all ages and backgrounds who share part of my journey. They are the ones who still struggle with literacy, who lack the basic skills they need to survive. They are the ones who cannot be forgotten or left behind — for their sakes and ours.

The second edition of *The Teacher Who Couldn't Read* may be riveting for people because of the intrigue and drama of a personal story of survival and getting by. It is a memoir of pain and hope and celebration. Writing it then and revisiting it now has been a challenging journey of telling the truth, admitting transgressions, dealing with shame, working through anger, seeking and bestowing forgiveness, sharing joy, being thankful, and imploring for help for others like me. Thank you for choosing to read this book. I hope it inspires you onward, to the *Bridge to Literacy*, to actively help others discover the liberty, independence, and opportunity that comes from being a full member of our literate society.

APPENDIX

Chapter 15

p. 208

- It was gratifying to learn that I wasn't the only one with this problem. Some people compensate by memorizing, some are just called "creative spellers," and others have a bad case, like mine.

- A more technical explanation says: "Research into the ability called auditory processing, phonological processing, phonological awareness, or phoneme segmentation shows that many people have trouble identifying sounds within words once they've heard the word." David Conway, *Help??? Help!!! Solving Learning Problems (Even Dyslexia)* (San Luis Obispo, Calif.: Pre Publishing, 1992), p. 49

p. 216

- Nanci Bell explained to me that a disorder in language comprehension is a weakness in creating the whole picture from what we read. For instance, when the main idea of the written or spoken word cannot be grasped, and only a few parts are understood, the whole concept is lost. It's like words and sentences being written on a blackboard, with someone erasing them so fast you can only understand parts of what are written.

- I began to learn that images are the means by which we connect to language. Individuals who have difficulty imaging language often say, "Words go in one ear and out the other." When they read or listen, they often grasp some facts but get lost after a few sentences.

- I heard people say, "I have to read each sentence three times to try to make it stay in my head, and then go on to the next sentence and do the same thing. It usually makes no sense at all when put together."

- What do we hear from the children and adults who have poor reading comprehension and oral language comprehension? The same word. *Frustration!* I'm not implying that life should be free of frustration. That's impossible.

But given a chance to get the necessary skills, we can break out of our inability to read or comprehend and live up to our potential as productive citizens.

– Nanci calls the learning process "visualizing and verbalizing," a developmental procedure that can be taught and that leads to a dramatic increase in comprehension skills. I learned early in life that I had a hard time expressing myself, so I unconsciously developed a visual language (analogies) to explain and express the ideas I wanted to convey. Educators would call this a coping skill. My verbalization was scattered, relating information out of sequence or jumping from one thought to another so that sometimes my listeners had to run with their minds and ears to catch what I meant.

– There are many people who can read, who have wide experiences and good educations, but who are unable to comprehend efficiently. Children who read well, according to Nanci, but have weak comprehension, are not usually termed dyslexic and placed in special reading classes. They are often misdiagnosed as not trying, inattentive, lazy, or unintelligent.

p. 218

– Phonological awareness is a key issue in the development of literacy. Research studies in the United States, as well as in Australia, England, Belgium, Sweden, Portugal, and Italy seem to show that this understanding of individual speech sounds and their order within words is the missing link in the solution of the illiteracy/dyslexia puzzle. Marilyn Adams, in researching for her book *Beginning to Read*, concluded that the discovery and documentation of the importance of phoneme awareness is the single most powerful advance in the science and pedagogy of reading in this century. Marilyn Adams, *Beginning to Read* (Cambridge, Mass., MIT Press, 1990.)

– In 1993, over $350 billion were spent on education in the United States. Even with the best efforts of teachers and parents, almost one out of three children in our schools experience moderate to severe reading dysfunction. These children become the learning disabled in the upper grades and many of them become adult illiterates. Money alone is not solving the problem.

Chapter 16

p. 232

- What about literacy in the workplace? In the 1960s, a person who could read at the fifth-grade level was considered literate. Since the mid-1970s, a sixth- to eighth-grade level was more commonly used. Today, a 12th-grade level is the most widely accepted standard in use by employers for the literate worker.

- Dr. Edward Gordon, author of *Closing of the Literacy Gap in American Business*, said, "Though some low-skill jobs will remain, by the year 2000 75 to 80 percent of all occupations will require at least 12th-grade skills and aptitudes. This means that 40 percent of all current U.S. employees will need to increase their literacy skills."[1]

- The Americans with Disabilities Act has made it illegal to discriminate in hiring, supervising, or promoting individuals on the basis of a handicap. Persons who are blind, deaf, or wheelchair-mobile represent only a small portion of the nation's disabled population. The largest single group of disabled — over 55 percent according to the Stanford Research Institute — are those who have specific learning disabilities.

- The U.S. Commerce Department reported that our economy experiences a $300 billion annual production loss due to adult-worker illiteracy. The CEOs of America's *Fortune* 500 corporations are beginning to recognize that this human resource problem is a serious threat to our economy and to America's ability to compete in the international marketplace.

- An officer in a large company said, "You can't train people if they can't read or write."

ENDNOTES

Chapter 13

1 Ann Bradford Mathias, "Senator's Wife Struggles with a Learning Disability," *People*, June 20, 1983. Quoted in Dorothy Ungerleider, *Reading, Writing, and Rage* (Rolling Hills Estates, Calif: Jalmar Press, 1985), p. ix.

2 Ungerleider, p. ix.

3 Barbara Prete and Gary E. Strong, *Literate America Emerging* (Sacramento, Calif: State Library Association, 1991) pp. 72, 73.

4 Walter Anderson, *Read with Me* (Boston: Houghton Mifflin Co., 1990), pp. 115, 116.

5 Ibid. p. 104-109.

6 Richard Woodbury, "A Convict's View: 'People Don't Want Solutions,'" *Time*, August 23, 1993, p. 33.

7 Edward Klein, "Everything Would Be Better if More People Could Read," *San Diego Union, Parade Magazine,* May 21, 1989.

8 National Center for Education Statistics, Adult Literacy in America (U.S. Department of Education, 555 New Jersey Ave., N.W., Washington, D.C., September, 1993).

9 Data compiled from the Adult Literacy in America Survey, (NALS report), 1993. Also, news release from the National Institute for Literacy, 800 Connecticut Ave., N.W., Suite 200, Washington, D.C. 20006.

Chapter 14

1 Adult Literacy in America (NALS report), 1993.

2 Michael Brunner, "Can Everyone Read?" Right to Read Report (Washington, D.C.: National Right to Read Foundation, March, 1993).

3 James B. Jacobson, "Is Your School Telling You the Truth," Right to Read Report (Washington, D.C.: National Right to Read Foundation, June, 1993).

4 Interview by the author with Dr. Patrick Groff, Professor of Education Emeritus, San Diego State University, and nationally known expert in reading development.

5 Isabel Meyers, *Gifts Differing* (Palo Alto, Calif.: Consulting Psychologists Press, Inc., 1980) p. 150.

6 M. Eeds-Kniep, *The Frenetic, Fanatic, Phonic Backlash* (Urbana, Ill.: Language Arts, 1979), p. 909.

Chapter 16

1 The International Dyslexia Association, "Frequently Asked Questions about Dyslexia," www.interdys.org/FAQ.htm

2 National Reading Panel, "National Reading Panel Reports Combination of Teaching Phonics, Word Sounds, Giving Feedback on Oral Reading Most Effective Way to Teach Reading," www.nationalreadingpanel.org/Press/press_rel_4_13_00_1.htm

3 Senator Paul Simon, from a speech given for the National Center for Family Literacy, Louisville, Ky. National Conference, April 18, 1993.

ABOUT THE AUTHOR

JOHN CORCORAN'S professional career represents a merger of his life as a teacher, real estate investor, his building and development experiences, and his passion for a literate America. His background in teaching demonstrates his commitment to sharing his knowledge and experience with others.

The Honorable John Corcoran was appointed to the National Institute for Literacy by President George H. W. Bush, was confirmed by the U.S. Senate, and subsequently served on the Board of the Institute under President Bush and President Clinton. He has testified before the U.S. Congress Subcommittee of Early Childhood Education and Family and to the Subcommittee on Oversight and Investigation for the Committee on Economic and Educational Opportunities. In addition, he has served on numerous advisory commissions and corporate boards, has been a member of the board of the San Diego Council on Literacy, and presently is a member of the Executive Board of the Literacy Network of Greater Los Angeles. John is also the author of the book *The Teacher Who Couldn't Read* originally published by Focus on the Family and currently by Kaplan Publishing.

John's responsibilities in the building and development process involve interfacing with investors, lenders, attorneys, accountants, governmental agencies, architects, engineers, contractors, and brokers. John's entrepreneurial spirit and management experience have been well represented in his various professional roles over the past 35 years.

John is also a nationally known and respected speaker and lecturer who has given presentations in 44 states, in Canada, and in Europe to students, professional and volunteer teachers, teacher candidates, service groups and organizations, policymakers, and prison inmates, as well as numerous small business and *Fortune* 500 companies. He has appeared on *20/20*, the *Oprah Winfrey Show*, *Larry King Live*, and *Phil Donahue*. In all, he has done over 200 radio and TV interviews. John was also the recipient of a Lifetime Achievement Award at the 2002 Literacy in Media Awards.

John formalized his literacy visions and, along with a diversified group of individual business and professional people, founded *The John Corcoran Foundation, Inc.* The Foundation's mission is:

> "To facilitate the eradication and prevention of adult illiteracy in America through the creation and dissemination of resources, training, mentoring, and public awareness through existing literacy organizational and educational programs."

John is presently the president of this nonprofit organization. He and his wife have lived in Oceanside, California, for over 40 years. They have two adult children and four grandchildren.